EMPLOYEE/EMPLOYER RIGHTS

EMPLOYEE/EMPLOYER RIGHTS
A guide for the British Columbia work force

Leslie Baker, LL.B.

Self-Counsel Press
(a division of)
International Self-Counsel Press Ltd.
Canada   U.S.A.

Printed in Canada

First edition: April, 1972
Tenth edition: February, 1995

Canadian Cataloguing in Publication Data
    Baker, Leslie.
    Employee/employer rights

    (Self-counsel legal series)
    Previous eds. by James E. Dorsey.
    ISBN 0-88908-946-9

    1. Labor laws and legislation — British Columbia — Popular works. I. Dorsey, James E., 1947-. Employee/employer rights. II. Title. III. Series.
    KEB399.Z82D67 1994 344.711'01   C94-910907-X

    KF3319.6.D67 1994

Self-Counsel Press
(a division of)
International Self-Counsel Press Ltd.
Head and Editorial Office
1481 Charlotte Road
North Vancouver, British Columbia V7J lHl

U.S. Address
1704 N. State Street
Bellingham, Washington 98225

CONTENTS

1
EMPLOYMENT STANDARDS

a. OVERVIEW

This chapter examines —

- (a) pre-employment protections,
- (b) conditions of work,
- (c) benefits (including maternity and parental leave), and
- (d) health and safety requirements in a workplace.

The rules discussed in this chapter apply to unionized and non-unionized workers and their employers. Most workers in B.C. are not unionized and are employed in small workplaces with five employees or less.

Minimum standards for many conditions of work are found in the Employment Standards Act. These are only minimums and better working conditions can be agreed upon by the employer and employee. For example, the act states that the minimum hourly wage for persons over 18 is $6.00. An employer can pay a higher hourly wage, but not a lower hourly wage.

Health and safety standards in the workplace are governed by the Workers' Compensation Act, as well as regulations that set standards for specific workers, such as agricultural workers and fishers.

The Employment Standards Branch, through the offices of the Ministry of Skills, Training, and Labour enforces the requirements of the act. Penalties, usually in the form of fines, may be imposed for violations. The complaint process and possible remedies for breaches of the employment standards are discussed in chapter 3.

b. WHO IS PROTECTED BY THE ACT?

The Employment Standards Act applies to most B.C. employers and employees. However, the following workers are exempt from the act's protections:

(a) Federal employees

(b) Independent contractors

(c) Professionals

(d) Students

(e) Casual workers, such as babysitters, who work less than 15 hours per week

1. Federal employees

Employees in the following industries are federal employees who are subject to the Canada Labour Code, not the B.C. Employment Standards Act:

(a) Works or undertakings that connect a province with another province or country. This category includes railways, bus operations, trucking, pipelines, ferries, tunnels, canals, and telegraph and cable systems.

(b) All extra-provincial shipping and shipping services, such as longshoring and stevedoring.

(c) Air transport, aircraft, and airports

(d) Radio and television broadcasting

(e) Most federal Crown corporations such as Canada Post

(f) Other operations declared to be for the general benefit of Canada or two or more provinces (e.g., certain designated grain elevators and feed warehouses).

The B.C. office of Labour Canada can be contacted for further information about the laws governing federal employees.

2. Independent contractors

Independent contractors are considered to be self-employed and therefore are not covered by the act. The independent contractor agrees to perform certain tasks for the owner of a business or industry and usually supplies his or her own tools and any other work-related necessities.

A truck driver who owns and operates his or her own truck, but works for a specific contractor, is an example of an independent contractor. It is sometimes difficult to determine if a worker is an independent or dependent contractor. A dependent contractor may provide his or her own tools, yet be under the supervision of an employer and be economically dependent, just like an employee. Therefore, dependent contractors are characterized as employees and are covered by the provisions of the Employment Standards Act.

Employers may prefer to characterize a worker as an independent contractor because there is no employer-employee relationship. There are no protections for the independent contractor under the act. For example, the relationship can be terminated without complying with any of the dismissal provisions that apply to employees. As well, the independent contractor, not the employer, is entirely responsible for payment of all taxes and other benefit requirements.

3. Professionals

Professionals and student professionals in training are exempted from coverage under the Employment Standards Act. The rationale for this exemption is that most professionals are self-employed and do not need hours of work and wage protections. Students in training for the following professions may need to work longer hours in order to learn their profession:

3

(a) An architect or an articled student architect

(b) A chartered accountant or a student chartered accountant

(c) A lawyer or articled law student

(d) A chiropractor

(e) A dentist

(f) A professional engineer or engineer in training

(g) An insurance agent, salesperson, or adjuster

(h) A land surveyor or articled student

(i) A physician

(j) A naturopath

(k) An optometrist

(l) A podiatrist

(m) A real estate salesperson or agent under the Real Estate Act

(n) A securities salesperson, or other person registered under section 21 of the Securities Act

(o) A veterinarian

(p) A forester

4. Other exempted persons

The final category of exempt persons includes students and some types of part-time workers.

(a) Students

Students are exempt if they are —

(a) employed at a school where they are enrolled,

(b) enrolled at a secondary school in a work study, work experience, or occupational study program, or

4

(c) enrolled in an occupational training program under the direction of an instructor approved by the Minister of Education.

(b) Sitters

A sitter is defined as a person employed in a private residence solely to provide the service of attending to a child, or to a disabled, infirm, or other person. A sitter who provides care for 15 hours or more per week to a child, elderly person, or a disabled person is entitled to full protection under the act.

This definition does not apply to a nurse, therapist, domestic, homemaker, or an employee of a business that provides these services or a day care facility. These workers are covered under the act.

(c) Income assistance recipients

Income assistance recipients are those who receive income assistance benefits and participate in the Incentive Allowance for Employment Programme, which permits certain part-time employment. They are exempted from the act.

(d) Participants in job creation projects

Anyone who participates in certain job creation projects and receives payments that are supplemental to unemployment insurance benefits is exempted from the act.

(e) Newspaper carriers

A carrier who works more than 15 hours per week delivering newspapers must receive the minimum hourly wage and other protections under the act. A carrier who attends school and works less than 15 hours per week is exempt.

A newspaper is defined to exclude advertising circulars and flyers that are sold or given away other than with a newspaper.

(f) Prison inmates

An inmate under the Correction Act who is working in a government co-operative work program is excluded from the B.C. Employment Standards Act.

5. Partially exempted workers

Other workers receive some, but not all, of the protections of the act. Persons such as artists and performers work in unique conditions and have only certain protections under the act, such as the right to the minimum wage.

The provisions concerning hours of work, annual vacation, termination of employment, and maternity and parental leave do not apply to the following:

(a) Musicians

(b) Performers

(c) Actors

(d) Nursing students training to be registered or practical nurses

(e) Auxiliary or volunteer fire fighters employed by a fire department organized to protect the public

There are other employees who receive only some of the act's protections. For example, a fisher is excluded from the hours of work provisions in recognition of the need for fishers to work very long hours during the fishing season.

c. PRE-EMPLOYMENT PROTECTIONS

Before a person obtains employment, he or she is protected against false promises and discrimination in the job interview and any false advertisements for employment.

1. False representations

The employer must not mislead a job applicant about basic work conditions. The act states that an employer —

shall not, by means of deceptive or false representations, advertising, or pretenses respecting

(a) the availability of a position,

(b) the nature of the work to be done,

(c) the wages to be paid for the work, or

(d) the conditions of employment

induce, influence, or persuade a person to become his or her employee, or to undertake work, or to make himself or herself available for work.

This means that an employer cannot make false promises about the nature of the employment. The prohibition against misrepresentations applies to the job interview and to any job advertisement. For example, an employer cannot advertise a commissioned sales position that pays $1 000 per week when the job really earns about $300 per week. Another example would be to promise an applicant for a live-in nanny position that the work requires only child care and no house cleaning, when the job actually involves both.

The procedure for filing a complaint is discussed in chapter 3. If an employment standards officer determines that an employer made false representations, the employer can be ordered to pay the complainant any expenses incurred as a result. For example, if a job applicant is misled about a job and moves in order to take the promised employment, the employer can be ordered to pay the applicant for any reasonable moving expenses.

2. Discrimination

The Human Rights Act prohibits any advertisement of employment from discriminating on the basis of race, colour, ancestry, place of origin, political belief, religion, marital status, family status, physical or mental disability, sex, sexual orientation, or age. The only exception to this requirement is that a limitation, specification, or preference for employment based on these factors may be used if it is based on a bona fide occupational requirement.

More details of this prohibition against discrimination are given in chapter 4.

3. How to find a job

There are commercial employment agencies and government employment agencies that can help people find employment. Advertisements in local papers are another source of potential jobs.

(a) Government employment assistance

The federal government operates Canada Employment Centres in many communities. These centres provide postings of available jobs and some job counselling.

The provincial government provides some assistance through the Ministry of Skills, Training, and Labour.

(b) Private employment agencies

Private employment agencies provide job placement services by recruiting, for a fee, employees for employers. The fee is paid by the employer, not the job applicants. These agencies usually specialize in a particular type of worker, such as professionals, nannies, casual labourers, and office workers.

Private employment agencies are regulated by the Employment Standards Act and must register under the act if they provide workers for more than one employer. They must also pay an annual registration fee of $100 to the Director of Employment Standards. The director can refuse to register, cancel, or suspend the registration of an agency if the agency does not comply with the following rules, or operates contrary to the best interest of employers or job applicants:

(a) An employment agency must keep these records in English for at least three years:

(i) the names and addresses of all employers for whom it provides a job placement service, and

(ii) the name, occupation, and address of every job applicant referred to an employer.

These records must be retained at the agency's B.C. place of business, so that they can be inspected by an officer if necessary.

(b) People who receive job referrals from an employment agency cannot be required to pay any fee for this service. The fees are paid only by the employer. This provision is an important protection for job applicants. If an agency requests, demands, or receives a fee from a person seeking employment, that fee can be recovered under the act in the same way as unpaid wages. Any person required to pay a fee for a job referral or information about possible employers should file a complaint under the act. This process is discussed in chapter 3.

An employment agency is also prohibited from demanding or paying a fee to another person to obtain work for any person. For example, an agency can't pay money to the human resources manager in a company in return for placing a person in that company. The agency can be fined up to $2 000 for this practice.

Employment agencies can be located through the Yellow Pages.

d. WAGES

The definition of wages includes more than a weekly pay cheque. Wages can be salary, commission, or any other compensation paid by an employer to an employee for services or labour. Wages can also be money required to be paid as a result of an order against the employer by the Director of Employment Standards.

9

1. Minimum wage

As of October 1, 1995, the minimum wage will increase to $7. Effective March 1, 1995, the minimum wage for persons under 18 will be eliminated and workers under 18 will be paid the same as adults. This increase will occur in two stages:

(a) March 1, 1995: minimum wage increased to $6.50 per hour, from the current rate of $6.

(b) October 1, 1995: minimum wage will be increased to $7 per hour.

Note: The minimum wage changes frequently so it is advisable to check with the Employment Standards Branch to determine the current minimum wage.

Some employees, due to the nature of their work, receive different minimum wages:

(a) A live-in homemaker: A person employed by a home-making services agency who provides homemaking services on a 24-hour-a-day basis and lives in the place where these services are given will be paid at the minimum wage for a maximum of ten hours per day.

(b) A domestic: A person employed in a private home to provide domestic services such as cleaning, child care, or gardening and who lives in the home will be paid at the minimum hourly wage. This replaces the minimum daily wage of $48. Overtime payment is necessary when the domestic works more than eight hours a day. These persons are often called "live-in nannies." Nannies who live out of the home are protected by the minimum wage requirements which apply to most employees.

(c) A resident caretaker: A person who lives in an apartment building that has more than eight suites and is employed as a caretaker, custodian, janitor, or manager of the apartment building is entitled to the minimum hourly wage, and to overtime payments after more than eight hours a day.

(d) A farm worker or horticultural worker: Currently, a worker who is paid on a daily basis receives $48 per day. Most farm workers are not paid on a daily basis, but on a piece work basis (see below). **Note:** It is expected that this method of payment will change as of March 1, 1995. However, changes to the current system are strongly opposed by farm owners.

2. Farm workers

Farm work is seasonal and very intensive. Farm workers usually work on a piece work basis. They are paid according to the gross volume or weight of the fruit, vegetable, or berry crop picked.

A notice must be posted in a conspicuous place on the farm which clearly states —

(a) the volume of the container,

(b) the volume or weight of fruit, vegetable, or berries required to fill the container, and

(c) the piece rate to be paid.

(For specific wage rates for farm workers, see chapter 2, section **b. 2.**)

3. Minimum hours of pay

In many work situations, employees are called into work on a daily basis as needed. Where an employee is called into work and there is no work available that day, the employee must be paid a minimum of two hours' pay for reporting to work. When an employee reports for a regular shift which is cancelled, the same two-hour minimum applies.

Once an employee begins to actually work and work then ceases, the employee must be paid four hours' worth of wages. This minimum daily pay applies even if work stops after a short time.

There are two exceptions to the daily guaranteed pay:

(a) If work is suspended for a reason beyond the employer's control, employees receive two, not four hours' wages. For example, employees begin work at a construction site, but due to heavy rain, work stops after one hour. These employees will be paid two hours' wages.

(b) If the employee is a student reporting to work on a regular school day, two hours' wages must be paid, not four, where the employee has commenced work.

4. When are wages paid?

All wages must be paid at least twice per month, and no later than eight days after each pay period.

Wages must be paid in the lawful currency of Canada and can be paid by cheque, bill of exchange, order to pay, or by direct deposit to the employee's bank account.

A written statement of wages must be provided to the employee. This pay slip must explain the wage rate, the deductions, hours worked, and any additional payments.

Educational employees are exempt from the requirement that all wages be paid semi-monthly. These employees include the following:

(a) Teachers employed in the public or private school system

(b) University and college teachers

(c) Administrative and support staff in educational facilities

5. Wage deductions

Deductions include income tax, unemployment insurance premiums, and Canada Pension Plan contributions. Employers are required by law to make these contributions to the government on behalf of the employee.

The employer and employee cannot agree to waive or reduce the amount of these deductions unless the employee completes a form (Form TD1), which states that the income will not place the employee in a taxable category. Inquiries should be made of the local office of Revenue Canada for further information.

Other wage deductions require the consent of the employee. These may include company pension deductions, medical and dental plan premiums, charitable donations, or union fees.

An employee who is required to pay support money under the Family Maintenance Enforcement Act may have assigned payment of that money to the employer. This means that, usually as the result of a court order against the employee, part of his or her wages are assigned or paid over to the dependants.

An employer cannot deduct money from the regular wages for employee error without the employee's consent. For example, a restaurant owner cannot deduct the cost of broken dishes from a waiter's pay cheque.

6. Wage payment when the employee disappears

When an employee fails to show up for work to claim wages or disappears without any forwarding address, the employer is still required to pay any unpaid wages. The wages must be paid to the Director of Employment Standards no later than 60 days after they were due.

The director will provide a receipt to the employer for the amount paid. The director holds these monies on behalf of the former employee and will pay them on proof of a proper claim.

The employer then has no further responsibility for unpaid wages to the former employee. An employer who does not make this wage payment to the director commits an offence.

e. HOURS OF WORK

The general rule is that an employee cannot work more than eight hours per day, or 40 hours per week, without payment of overtime pay. However, there are several exceptions to this rule.

1. Split shifts

Some workplaces, such as restaurants and other hospitality service industries, use split shifts as usual working days. A split shift is a regular work day interrupted by rest periods, for which the employee is not paid. A split shift can only extend for 12 hours in total, including these rest periods. There is no entitlement to overtime so long as the maximum hours of work within the 12-hour period does not exceed eight hours.

There are many exceptions to this rule, including bus operators, ambulance drivers, police officers, college teachers, and fire fighters. See section **f.3.** for a complete list of occupations that are exempted from this "12-hour rule."

The exceptions recognize that there are many occupations, such as police officer, that require employees to work long hours during emergency situations. Other occupations, including college teaching, need more flexibility in terms of hours of work than the standard rule allows.

2. Notice

Notice of work hours must be posted in the workplace where employees can read it. The notice must state the following:

(a) the hours when work begins and ends,

(b) shift hours, where applicable, and

(c) eating periods.

3. Change in work schedule

Employers must give employees 24 hours' notice of a change in work schedule unless the change will provide the employee with overtime pay.

14

The employer and employee can mutually agree to vary this requirement and should request an exemption from this rule from the director of employment standards.

4. Excessive work hours

Employees may be asked by their employer to work long hours that are harmful to their health or safety. Should a complaint be made to the Employment Standards Branch, an officer can order that the employer limit the daily or weekly hours of work to eight in a day or 40 in a week.

A copy of this order must be posted in the workplace where all employees can read it. It is an offence to violate this order. If the order is violated and the employer continues to demand that employees work excessive hours, the officer can —

(a) vary the overtime rate to triple, quadruple, or more, or

(b) retroactively vary the rate of overtime to the date of the first order.

5. Special industries

Dangerous and stressful occupations are governed by special rules that require limited work hours that cannot be exceeded. Mining, fire fighting, and smelter work requires shifts of a maximum of eight hours in total, except for emergency situations.

f. REST PERIODS

The act guarantees daily and weekly rest periods for the health and safety of the employee.

1. Meal breaks

Employees are entitled to a meal break of one-half hour after a maximum of five hours of work. The employer is not required to pay for meal breaks, although many do pay for this period of time. The employer and employee can agree to vary this mandatory meal break and must request variation from the director of employment standards. Failure to grant a meal break is an offence punishable by a maximum fine of $2 000.

Coffee breaks are not required by law, although many employers allow one or two short breaks per shift.

See section **4.** below for the list of exceptions to the meal break entitlement.

2. Daily rest period

Employees are entitled to an eight-hour period free from work between each shift. In an emergency, the employer can request that the employees take a shorter rest period.

3. Weekly rest period

The weekly rest period is simply the days off from the job. An employee is entitled to a 32-hour consecutive period free from work each week. Usually, this period is the weekend, but it can vary according to the workplace demands.

If a worker is required to work during his or her rest period, he or she must be paid double time. Failure to pay this overtime rate is a punishable offence with a fine of up to $2 000.

The following workers are not covered by this provision:

(a) Live-in homemakers and domestic workers

(b) Farm and horticultural workers

(c) Bus operators

(d) Truck drivers or helpers

(e) Motorcycle operators

(f) Kitchen or recreation workers employed in an indus-trial undertaking located in a rural area (logging camps, mining camps)

(g) Ambulance drivers or attendants

These employees may be required to work with less than a 32-hour consecutive rest period and will not be paid overtime for these hours.

4. Overtime

The employer can ask employees to work overtime. Employees may only refuse to work overtime if the number of hours would threaten health and safety or is excessive. Most employees are entitled to additional compensation called overtime pay when they work more than the standard number of hours.

An employer must pay overtime to an employee who works more than eight hours in a day or more than 40 hours per week (excluding the hours that are in excess of eight hours per day).

Overtime is calculated at two rates: time-and-a-half and double time, according to the number of hours of overtime worked in a day or in a week. The pay rate is one-and-a-half times the regular rate for the first 11 hours in a day, or from 40 to 48 hours per week. The pay rate is double the regular rate for any overtime worked over 11 hours in a day or 48 hours per week.

For example, an employee works the following hours:

Monday:	9 hours
Tuesday:	9 hours
Wednesday:	12 hours
Thursday:	8 hours
Friday:	9 hours

This employee has worked 47 hours in total. The wages would be calculated at 40 hours at the regular hourly rate, one hour at double time (the one hour on Wednesday in excess of 11 hours), and six hours at time-and-a- half (for the remaining hours worked in the week, up to the 47 hours in total).

Overtime must also be paid in two other situations:

(a) Where a work week contains a general holiday, overtime pay is calculated after an employee works a 32-hour week, not the usual 40 hours. (General holidays are defined in section **g.** below.)

(b) Where an employee does not receive a 32-hour rest period during a week, overtime pay is due, calculated at double time

Some occupations are excluded from the protections concerning maximum hours of work, payment for overtime, and hours free from work, including meal breaks. These are as follows:

(a) Fishing or hunting guides

(b) Persons, other than percussion drill or diamond drill operators or their helpers, who are employed in staking, line cutting, geological mapping, geochemical sampling and testing, geophysical surveying, or manual stripping activities in the course of exploration for minerals other than oil and gas

(c) Persons employed by a board of school trustees of a school district as a teacher, substitute teacher, part-time instructor, noon hour supervisor, teacher's aide, or supervision aide

(d) Part-time instructors employed by a public institution that provide training in a trade, occupation, vocation, or hobby

(e) Managers primarily employed as a supervisor of other employees, or as executives

(f) Persons employed on a commercial fishing boat or vessel

(g) Persons employed as guards, fire wardens, or camp persons in a commercial fishing operation,

(h) Person employed as emergency fire fighters or fire wardens or on a towboat other than a boom boat, a dozer boat, or a camp tender, in connection with a commercial fishing operation

(i) Police officers employed by a municipal police board

(j) Fire fighters employed by a paid fire department. (Fire fighters are entitled to overtime if they are hired to fight forest fires.)

(k) Commercial travellers who, during their travels, buy or sell goods from samples, catalogues, price lists, or other forms of advertising material

g. GENERAL HOLIDAYS

In B.C. there are nine general or statutory holidays per year:

(a) New Year's Day

(b) Good Friday

(c) Victoria Day

(d) Canada Day

(e) British Columbia Day

(f) Labour Day

(g) Thanksgiving Day

(h) Remembrance Day

(i) Christmas Day

The basic rule is that employees receive a holiday with pay on these general holidays, or another day with pay, or receive overtime for working on a general holiday.

An employer can require an employee to work on one of these statutory holidays. However, the employee must be paid overtime pay or receive another day off with pay, to be provided before the employee's next vacation or termination of employment.

19

Should a general holiday fall on a non-working day, for example on a Sunday, the employee must receive another day off with pay. This paid day off must be provided before the employee's next vacation, or on termination of employment, whichever is first.

Employees who have worked less than the standard work week in the four weeks prior to a general holiday must receive holiday pay on a pro-rated basis. This means that they are paid a percentage of the holiday pay owed to a full-time employee. Farm workers are not entitled to paid general holidays.

h. ANNUAL VACATIONS

1. When is an employee eligible?

Employees must work one year before they are entitled to a paid annual vacation. They are then entitled to two weeks' vacation after one year of employment. After five years of employment, an employee must receive three weeks of paid annual vacation.

The first annual vacation must be given within ten months of the employee's anniversary date. For example, if an employee begins work January 1, 1995, she is entitled to her first annual vacation after January 1, 1996, which is her anniversary date. This vacation must be granted within ten months of the anniversary date; that is, prior to November 1, 1996.

Employers have the right to schedule the vacation at a time which is convenient. However, they cannot require employees to take their vacation time in periods of less than one week. An employee can, with the employer's consent, take the vacation in shorter periods.

Employers may also use a common anniversary date for the purposes of calculating annual vacation, and if the employer does this, employees are entitled to the appropriate proportion of the annual vacation if they have not completed a year of employment.

2. Vacation pay

An employer must pay annual vacation pay to each employee calculated on the employee's total wages for the year at a rate of at least 2% for each week of vacation. That means for employees with less than five years employment, the annual vacation pay rate is at least 4% of their total earnings, and for employees with five or more years of employment, the rate is 6% of their total earnings.

The employer cannot reduce the amount of vacation pay if an employee takes a longer vacation than he or she is entitled to under the act.

Failure to pay the necessary amount of vacation pay at the time required is an offence and the employer can be fined up to $2 000.

An employee who has worked for less than one year and is terminated must receive vacation pay of 4% of the gross earnings for the period of employment. For example, if a worker is terminated after six months and earned $18 000 for those six months, the vacation pay will be $720.

An employee who has worked for more than one year is entitled to any unpaid vacation pay for the last year of employment. This amount is calculated according to when he or she was last paid vacation pay. For example, if the employee was terminated one month after returning from holidays, vacation pay is simply 4% or 6% of the employee's gross earnings for the last month of employment.

3. Payment

Vacation pay must be paid in one payment at least seven days prior to the beginning of the annual vacation, or, as discussed above, prior to termination of employment. The "one payment" rule means that if an employee and employer agree that the employee can take one or two days of vacation separate from the regular vacation period, the entire year's vacation pay must be paid at that time.

For example, an employee entitled to two weeks' vacation takes one day of that two-week period early in the spring to attend a friend's wedding. According to the act, that employee must receive the entire year's vacation pay seven days prior to the one-day brief vacation.

i. MATERNITY AND PARENTAL LEAVE

The act guarantees new parents two benefits: leave from their job after the birth or adoption of a child, and job protection during the leave period.

There are two types of leave provided to parents under the act: maternity leave, which is available for new mothers, and parental leave, which can be taken by either parent and shared by both of them. Maternity leave is taken directly before and after the birth of the child. Parental leave can be taken immediately following the end of the maternity leave, in the case of the mother (unless the employer and employee agree otherwise) and in the case of the father, any time during the 52 weeks after the birth or adoption.

1. Maternity leave provisions

All female employees are entitled to 18 weeks' maternity leave without pay before and after their child's birth, and job protection during the same period. The employer is not required to pay for maternity leave. However, the employee may be eligible for U.I.C. benefits during maternity leave.

Maternity leave begins 11 weeks prior to the estimated date of birth, or on a later date, if the employee so requests.

To request maternity leave, the employee must make a written request to the employer at least four weeks prior to the anticipated date of leave. The request must include a doctor's certificate that states that she is pregnant and estimates the birth date.

In the case of premature birth or an unexpected termination of pregnancy, the employee may be unable to request maternity leave in advance. In this case, she is entitled to six weeks' maternity leave. A doctor's certificate is required.

The general rule is that maternity leave may not end until six weeks after the birth of the child. This rule is to ensure the health of the new mother and infant. However, an earlier return to work can be granted. To request a return to work before the expiry of the six-week period, the employee must make a written request to the employer at least one week prior to the anticipated return date and include a doctor's certificate which states she is able to work.

An employer can require an employee to begin maternity leave where her duties cannot reasonably be performed due to the pregnancy. However, the onus is on the employer to prove that the pregnancy substantially prevents performance of the job. This burden of proof is often difficult for an employer to satisfy. Should the job be difficult for a pregnant employee, the employer should consider finding other duties in the workplace which can be performed by the employee.

The 18-week period of leave can be extended for six more weeks if the employee cannot return to work for health reasons. Her job continues to be protected during this period.

To request an extension of maternity leave, the employee must make a written request to the employer and include a doctor's certificate which states that she is unable to work for health reasons. This provision also applies to a woman who is unable to return to work for health reasons after a miscarriage.

2. Parental leave

In addition to maternity leave, the act recognizes that both parents want and need to spend time with a new child. Therefore, the act provides for parental leave as well as maternity leave. All employees who become parents are entitled to an unpaid parental leave for a period of up to 12 weeks. Again, job security is guaranteed during this leave period. Parental leave is unpaid, but employees may be eligible for U.I.C. benefits.

Natural mothers, natural fathers, and adoptive mothers and fathers can receive parental leave. The leave must be taken within 52 weeks of the child's birth or adoption. The date that it begins depends on the relationship of the parent to the child:

(a) It begins immediately after maternity leave expires for a natural mother (unless the employer and employee agree otherwise)

(b) It begins any time after the birth of the child and within 52 weeks of the child's birth for a natural father

(c) It begins any time after the adoption of the child, for the adopting mother and father, and within 52 weeks of the date the adoptive child comes into the actual care of the mother or father

Both parents are eligible for parental leave. A request should be made in writing, at least four weeks prior to the date of leave. Where the employee is a natural parent, a doctor's certificate stating the anticipated birth date, or actual birth date is needed, and where the employee is an adoptive parent, evidence of the adoption is needed.

A natural mother is entitled to a maximum of 32 weeks combined maternity and parental leave, taken in one consecutive period. This is unpaid leave. Her job will be protected during the entire leave period.

3. Job protection

One of the most important provisions of the act is job protection. An employee who takes leave, either maternity or parental, has the right to return to his or her former job, or a job of equal position.

Therefore, an employer cannot terminate or fire an employee who takes a lawful maternity or parental leave. As well, the employer cannot change a condition of employment during this period. For example, a senior computer programmer takes maternity leave and returns to find she has been demoted to a junior position. The employer cannot change her position without her written consent. In this case, the employer would be required to reinstate the employee to her former position or offer her another position of the same seniority.

Should an employer either terminate such an employee or change any condition of employment, the burden is on the employer to prove that these changes were not in any way related to the maternity or parental leave. The act provides remedies in the form of job reinstatement, lost wages, or financial compensation to an employee whose employer contravenes these provisions.

4. Other benefits

Other rights attached to maternity and parental leave include the following:

(a) The period of leave is included as employment in calculating the annual vacation.

(b) The period of leave is included as employment in calculating job seniority

(c) Any wage and benefit increases granted to similar employees during the period of leave must be paid to the returning employee.

(d) All benefits, including pension and medical benefits, may continue. Where the benefits are paid solely by the employer, the premiums must be paid by the employer during the leave period. Where the benefits are paid jointly by the employer and the employee, if the employee chooses to continue to pay his or her share of the premiums, employers must also continue to pay their share of the premiums

(e) Where the employer suspends or discontinues operations during the period of leave, if the employer subsequently resumes operations, the employee who was on leave must receive all wage and benefit increases granted to similar employees during their leave period.

5. Remedies

An employer who terminates an employee on lawful maternity or parental leave can be ordered to reinstate that employee. An order to pay wages that the wrongfully terminated worker should have received can also be made against the employer.

j. SICK LEAVE

There is no provision for paid sick leave under the Employment Standards Act. Employers may provide sick leave, paid or unpaid, but this is a matter that is negotiated between the employer and the employee.

It is important for a new employee to discuss this issue when starting a new job in order to understand the employer's sick leave policies.

k. TIME OFF TO VOTE

All employees who are eligible to vote in federal or provincial elections are entitled to four consecutive hours, while the polls are open, to vote. For example, if normal office hours are 9:00 a.m. to 5:00 p.m. and the polls are open until 8:00 p.m., all employees are entitled to leave at 4:00 p.m. This gives the employees four clear hours, from 4:00 p.m. until 8:00 p.m., in which to vote.

The "four-hour rule" applies in both federal and provincial elections. There is no right to time off to vote in municipal elections.

Any time off to vote must be granted at the employer's convenience, so long as the employee has four clear hours in which to vote. Any time off work must be with pay.

Any employer who, directly or indirectly, refuses or by intimidation and undue influence interferes with this right is guilty of an offence under the Canada Elections Act, if it is a federal election, or the Election Act of B.C., if it is a provincial election.

l. HEALTH AND SAFETY

Various acts govern health and safety standards in the workplace, including the Health Act and the Workplace Act. The Workers' Compensation Board oversees the enforcement of health and safety standards. Regulations set out specific standards for various workplaces. A board officer can inspect any factory, office, or shop to ensure the health, safety, or comfort of workers during regular working hours.

The Workplace Act applies to factories, shops, offices, and home work. Conditions of work regulated by the act and its occupational environment regulations include illumination, temperature, air quality, washroom facilities, and lunchroom facilities.

1. Lunchrooms

A lunchroom in a factory or office must be a self-contained room with an appropriate number of square feet per number of persons working on a shift at any one time (see below). The minimum size of a lunchroom is 60 square feet. A lunchroom may be necessary in a shop, if an inspector so directs.

Number of people	Square feet per person
25 and less	12
26 to 74	10
75 to 149	7
150 to 499	6
500 and more	5

The other health and safety requirements for a lunchroom are as follows:

(a) The floor is resistant to water.

(b) The ceiling and walls are easily cleaned and have a light-colored, washable surface. The ceiling and walls must be kept clean.

(c) The room must not have an exit that leads into a washroom.

(d) The light is shielded (not a bare bulb) and gives the equivalent of 30 foot candles of illumination, measured 30 inches above the floor.

(e) The minimum temperature of the room must be 21°C.

(f) The windows should equal one-tenth of the floor area in size.

(g) The windows which open should equal at least 5% of the floor area in size, unless there is adequate mechanical exhaust to the outdoors which provides at least six air changes per hour. This regulation can be changed by order of an inspector.

(h) The room has a two-compartment sink that provides hot and cold water, unless an inspector orders otherwise.

(i) There must be an enclosed cupboard to contain food, dishes, and utensils.

(j) Tables with impervious top surfaces and chairs equipped with back rests must be provided.

(k) Appliances to heat or cool drinks and sufficient dishes and utensils should be available unless an inspector directs otherwise.

(l) Waste receptacles with self-closing lids are provided, emptied daily, and kept in a clean and sanitary condition.

(These requirements are found in Division 12 of the Occupational Environment Regulations.)

2. Washrooms

Separate washrooms for male and female employees are necessary in every building used as a factory, office, or shop. These washrooms must have separate approaches and signs that clearly indicate whether they are for men or women.

The number of water closets in the washrooms depends on whether the workplace is a factory, office, or shop. Every building used as a factory must provide:

(a) one water closet and one urinal for every 25 male employees

(b) one water closet for every nine female employees or fewer

(c) one washbasin or other satisfactory washing facility that provides hot and cold water for every 15 employees or fewer.

Where there is shift work and the maximum number of employees on any one shift is less than six, only one water closet is required.

Every shop or office must provide:

(a) one water closet for every nine employees

(b) two water closets for ten to 24 employees

(c) one water closet for each additional 25 employees

(d) one washbasin that provides hot and cold water for every two water closets or urinals

Where two or more water closets are required for ten or more male employees, half of the water closets can be replaced by urinals.

3. Toiletries

Some industrial workplaces do not have the washroom facilities in the workplace. Certain toiletries must be provided, including clean towels, soap, and safe drinking water.

4. Room temperature

The lunchroom must be a minimum of 21°C and the washrooms, dressing rooms, locker rooms, and restrooms must be a minimum of 20°C. The temperature is measured at five feet above the floor.

5. Accommodation for clothing

Where employees wear uniforms or other clothing specifically required for their employment, the employer must provide some suitable storage for employees' regular clothing. An inspector may order that a dressing room and/or individual lockers be provided.

6. First aid kit

The Workers' Compensation Act requires all employers to maintain specified first aid equipment and services on the job site. If an employee is injured while working, the employer must provide free transportation to a physician or a hospital.

m. MISCELLANEOUS CONDITIONS

1. Seniority

The act has no rules concerning protection of seniority rights. An employee must try to negotiate seniority rights with the employer.

Unionized employees usually have seniority rights in the collective agreement with the employer.

2. Uniforms and special clothing

An employer who requires employees to wear special clothing must:

(a) provide the clothing, and

(b) clean, repair, and launder the clothing.

The employee cannot be charged for the purchase of the clothing or for its cleaning and upkeep.

The act provides a specific remedy when an employer wrongly deducts money from an employee for clothing. Any money deducted from an employee's wages is deemed to be wages owing to the employee and can be collected from the employer.

3. Falsifying an employment record

It is a criminal offence to falsify an employment record with an intent to deceive. This offence includes any false representation concerning hours worked, such as punching a time clock with the wrong time. It also includes any misrepresentations about previous employment given by a job applicant to a prospective employer.

The penalty for this offence is a maximum fine of $2 000 or imprisonment of up to six months or both. As well, the person convicted receives a criminal record.

n. TERMINATION

Employment can end in several ways: the employee can be dismissed (the term used for being fired or laid off), or the employee can quit. The focus of this section is on the rights of a dismissed employee and the obligations of the employer.

Termination of employment can be for cause, or without cause. The distinction is important because an employee who is dismissed from a job without cause is entitled to severance pay or notice.

Severance pay is the greater of the employee's average or weekly wages for the eight-week period prior to the termination of employment. It does not include any overtime pay earned in that period.

After six months of employment, an employee is entitled to two weeks of notice or severance pay. After three years of employment, an employee is entitled to three weeks of notice or severance pay. For every year of employment after the third year, an employee is entitled to another week of notice or severance pay, up to a maximum of eight weeks. In some cases, the court may order a longer period of notice than that required by the Employment Standards Act where the employee was wrongfully dismissed.

An employer must give written notice of termination to the employee. Verbal notice is not sufficient.

1. Dismissal with just cause

An employee owes certain duties to the employer and can be dismissed or fired if these duties are breached. These duties are implied in any employment contract and require an employee to serve the employer faithfully, honestly, and diligently.

Just cause means that the employee has breached the terms of the employment contract with the employer and can be dismissed without any obligation on the part of the employer. An employee dismissed with just cause is not entitled to notice or severance pay.

(a) Misconduct

An employee should not misconduct himself or herself at work. Examples of misconduct include immoral conduct, intoxication, and theft of the employer's property.

The B.C. Court of Appeal ruled in 1994 that an employer is always justified in firing a dishonest employee, since dishonesty in any amount is a breach of the condition of "faithful service." It does not matter if the amount of property stolen from the employer is very small in value.

(b) Disloyalty

The B.C. Supreme Court found in 1993 that a former employee who frequently made critical comments about his employers was dismissed with cause. The former employee worked in association with his employers in a dental specialty practice. The court concluded that he criticized his employers' competence, training, and facilities to other persons, including staff. This disloyalty justified his dismissal for cause.

An employee should follow all reasonable and lawful orders of the employer. Employees are not required to follow orders that may endanger their life or safety. The exception to this rule is a job, such as mining, which specifically contains an element of risk.

Employees should not be insulting or rude to the employer. While one isolated act of rudeness may be insufficient cause for dismissal, a pattern of such conduct may well be valid cause for dismissal.

(c) Incompetence

An employee must perform the job competently, with care and attention. One isolated minor act of neglect will not be sufficient cause for dismissal, but consistent negligence can give cause for dismissal.

However, any concerns about the ability of an employee to correctly perform a job should be expressed early in the employment relationship so that the employee has an opportunity to improve work performance. Allegations of incompetence that are made against a long-time employee will be unlikely to provide cause for dismissal.

2. Dismissal for other reasons

There are other situations in which employment terminates, but neither the employee nor the employer is at fault. Therefore, no notice or severance pay is necessary.

These situations are —

(a) Where an employee works temporarily,

(b) Where an employee is employed for a specific length of time

(c) Where an employee is employed to complete specific work within a time period that does not exceed 12 months,

(d) Where an employee has been offered and refused reasonable alternate employment by the employer

(e) Where the employment contract cannot be performed because of some unforeseen circumstance or event

One example of an "unforeseen circumstance or event" is when the physical circumstances make the job impossible to perform. For example, an employee is hired to construct a hydroelectric station; the river floods and the project is cancelled.

3. Dismissal without cause

An employer may dismiss an employee without cause, so long as proper notice or severance pay is provided. Severance pay is salary in lieu of notice. For example, if an employee has worked for two years, he or she is entitled to either two weeks' notice that the job is terminated or two weeks' salary.

4. What is proper notice?

The length of notice depends on the time an employee works for an employer. The purpose of reasonable notice is to allow the employee to conduct a job search and find alternate employment while still employed.

The act provides that an employee is entitled to two weeks' notice after a six-month employment period, and after three years or more, an additional week for each year of employment up to a maximum of eight weeks.

However, the minimum statutory notice in the act is applicable to situations where the dismissed employee's chances of finding another job are maximized. Former employees can ask the court to fix a longer notice period. Severance pay is calculated on the basis of the notice period.

Factors that determine the proper length of notice include years of service, the age of the employee, the level of responsibility held by the employee, the prospects for similar employment, and whether the dismissed employee was hired after being persuaded to leave secure employment elsewhere.

The court can also consider the economic conditions in a particular industry and any resulting lack of employment opportunities.

Example:

In 1993, the B.C. Supreme Court considered the case of a lumber sorter who worked at a sawmill for nine months. The employee worked full-time for only the final five months. Under the act, the dismissed employee was entitled to two weeks' notice after working full-time for six months. The court awarded a notice period of three weeks, noting that the forest industry was in a depressed economic situation.

In another 1993 decision, the B.C. Court of Appeal considered what would be reasonable notice to a senior sales manager employed in a sawmill equipment firm for his entire adult life. The court found that due to the former manager's age, there was a poor prospect of alternate employment. The appropriate notice period was held to be 15 months.

5. Constructive dismissal

Constructive dismissal is a legal term which means that the employment relationship ends through the conduct of the employer. In such cases, even though employees were not fired, they can infer termination of their employment and recover reasonable notice or salary in lieu of notice.

Constructive dismissal occurs through the extension of a temporary layoff or a substantial change in the conditions of employment.

(a) Temporary layoff

Some industries do not provide uninterrupted employment due to seasonal fluctuations in demand. Temporary layoffs do not constitute termination of the employment relationship if the interruption of employment is less than 13 weeks.

However, a temporary layoff becomes termination when the time period exceeds 13 weeks. The only exception is where an employer wants to recall the employee within a greater length of time and receives consent from the Director of Employment Standards.

Once a temporary layoff becomes termination, the employee is entitled to severance pay equal to the period of notice that would be required if the employee was working at the time.

(b) Change in employment conditions

An employee who resigns is not entitled to severance pay, so the employer, in certain cases, changes the conditions of employment to such an extent that the employee is discouraged from continuing to work.

For example, an employee works as the manager of human resources in a large company and supervises five junior employees. The employer wants the employee to quit but does not want to pay severance pay. The employer informs the employee that his or her new job is as junior clerk to the new manager of human resources. Such conduct constitutes a substantial change of the conditions of employment and the employer will be responsible for payment of severance.

Many changes are considered to be a fundamental change of the employment contract, including —

(a) a change in the job structure which reduces responsibility,

(b) a decrease in salary,

(c) the addition of new and different responsibilities, without the employee's consent, and

(d) demotion to a less responsible job.

Transfers, either geographic, to another job site, or within one location, may or may not be a substantial alteration of an employment condition. Recent cases have recognized the employer's need to change employees' positions for proper business purposes, and in particular, transfers which are necessitated by economic reasons.

Example:

The B.C. Supreme Court held that an employee who was the office manager was constructively dismissed when the employer cancelled the employee's signing authority on all bank accounts. The employer also changed the locks so the employee could access the work premises only during working hours. This conduct showed a loss of confidence in the employee who was then entitled to severance pay.

o. GROUP TERMINATIONS

The act has special rules concerning the termination of groups of 50 or more employees, which are designed to protect the employees by giving them a greater notice period than an individual employee. Group terminations usually occur where an employer must cease operations at an industrial site.

When the employer intends to terminate the employment of 50 or more employees at a single location within a two-month period, advance notice must be given to the following:

(a) each employee whose employment will be terminated,

(b) the trade union certified to represent such employees,

(c) the trade union that is recognized by the employer as the employees' bargaining agent, and

(d) the Minister of Skills, Training, and Labour

Depending on the number of employees whose employment will terminate, the amount of notice required varies:

(a) At least eight weeks is required before the date of the first termination if the number of employees does not exceed 100.

(b) At least 12 weeks is required before the date of the first termination if the number of employees does not exceed 300.

(c) At least 16 weeks before the date of the first termination if the number of employees exceeds 300.

There are exceptions to the notice requirement, the most notable of which is for workers in the construction industry. Other employees excluded from the notice provision are employees discharged for just cause, workers employed under a temporary work arrangement, workers employed for a definite term or for specific work, or workers employed where it is impossible to perform the job due to an unforeseeable event or circumstance.

p. REFERENCE LETTERS

There is no obligation on the part of an employer to provide a reference letter to a terminated employee. However, where the employment relationship ends because of economic or other reasons, and not the employee's conduct, it is useful for the employee to request a reference letter.

q. PUBLIC SERVICE EMPLOYEES

Many provincial public service employees are unionized and their rights and duties are governed by the principles discussed in chapter 6.

Non-unionized public service employees are protected by the Employment Standards Act. A particular occupation may also be regulated by a specific act. For example, the School Act has some rules concerning the employment of teachers.

2

SPECIAL EMPLOYMENT SITUATIONS

a. YOUTH EMPLOYMENT

There are special rules concerning the employment of young persons. These rules are designed to protect young people from working long hours or in environments that could be physically harmful.

Young persons under the age of 15 require a permit in order to work part-time or during school holidays. They cannot work full-time unless they have completed all locally available schooling.

Regulations state that people under 15 must attend school unless —

(a) they have completed the course available at any public school within 4.8 kilometres, and

(b) the local school board has not provided transportation available within 3.2 kilometres of the young person's home to a higher grade of school.

A young person under 15 can work after school, weekends, and during school holidays, but only after obtaining a permit from the Ministry of Skills, Training, and Labour. This permit is necessary for most employment such as clerking in a retail store or working in a restaurant. No permit is necessary for babysitting or employment at school.

1. How to obtain a work permit

To obtain a permit, the following conditons must be met:

(a) the youth's parent or guardian must give written consent,

(b) the school must agree that the employment will not adversely affect the youth's education if the request is made during the school year, and

(c) the work must not be dangerous or detrimental to the health of the young person.

Each permit application is considered by an officer with the employment standards board who may issue a permit with conditions of employment attached. For example, if the young person is in school, the permit may limit the number of hours that can be worked in the evenings and on the weekend.

2. Farm work for young persons

Young people age 12 to 14 may want to work harvesting fruit, berry, and vegetable crops. A permit must be applied for and the following conditions must be met:

(a) The youth's parent or guardian must give written consent,

(b) The youth's school must agree that the employment will not adversely affect his or her education if the request is made during the school year,

(c) and the work may not be dangerous or detrimental to the health of the young person.

As for work conditions during the harvest, the employer of young persons must comply with these conditions:

(a) No child can work in the vicinity of pesticides or pesticide containers.

(b) No child can work in a field recently sprayed with pesticides until it is safe to re-enter.

(c) Personal hygiene facilities must be available near the work location.

(d) No child must work with or near flammable products.

(e) No child must work with or near machinery, vehicles, or mechanical equipment.

(f) Adult supervision must be provided at the work location.

(g) No child can work later than 6:30 p.m.

3. Mining work for young persons

The mining industry is more closely regulated, due to concerns about safety. No person under 18 may work either underground or at the working face of an open-pit mine. The one exception is a person who is 17 years of age and in a training program approved by the chief inspector.

4. Penalties

Employers must comply with regulations concerning employment of young people. It is an offence to employ a young person under 15 without the consent of the Director of Employment Standards, or to employ a young person under 15 under conditions prohibited by the Director of Employment Standards.

Parents or guardians commit an offence if they consent to the employment of a person under 15 and have not obtained the permission of the director.

Should an employer be prosecuted or charged with an offence, the onus is on the employer to prove the person is not under 15. The physical maturity of the young person is not a defence.

b. FARM LABOUR

Special rules govern farm workers and their employers. Growers require a large number of temporary workers on a short-term basis when a crop is ready for harvesting. The work is seasonal and very intensive. Growers often choose to use the services of farm labour contractors rather than hire the large number of workers necessary themselves.

Therefore, the grower who needs seasonal workers contracts with a farm labour contractor who employs the workers directly and is responsible for paying wages. Wages are usually paid not on an hourly basis, but per weight of the crop picked or harvested. Farm workers paid on a piece work basis are not protected by the minimum wage provisions.

A farm labour contractor is defined as an employer of the workers who are hired to plant, cultivate, or harvest any horticultural or agricultural product, for or under the direction of another person. The grower may instruct the workers but is not in an employment relationship with them.

The role of the contractor is to select and hire the farm workers and transport them to the work site.

1. Obtaining a farm labour contractor licence

The Director of Employment Standards licenses all farm labour contractors. The purpose of the licence process is to ensure that those who hire farm workers do not exploit them. The farm labour contractor must provide evidence of good character and financial stability, so that the employees will have some guarantees concerning payment of monies earned.

The licence is valid only for one year and must be renewed annually. Farm labour contractors are required to carry the licence when carrying on business, either with employees or farmers.

The Director of Employment Standards must issue a licence if the following conditions are satisfied by the applicants:

(a) They provide a written statement setting out their past experience as a farm labour contractor and details of the proposed business

(b) Evidence of their character, competence, and responsibility

(c) Evidence, through an oral or written examination, or both, of a satisfactory knowledge of the Employment Standards Act and regulations

(d) They provide a written statement with the names and addresses of all persons financially interested in the proposed business. For example, partners, associates, directors, or shareholders must be included, with details of the amount of their interest in the business.

(e) A security deposit for wages or a bond in an amount required by the director

(f) Payment of the annual licence fee of $150

Where the licence is issued to a corporation, any changes in either the shareholders or directors of that corporation require that a new licence is applied for within seven days of the change.

Licences may not be transferred from one person or corporation to another. The licence can be cancelled or suspended where the farm labour contractor gives a false statement or misrepresentation in the licence application, or does not comply with any rule concerning the health or safety of the workers.

2. Duties of the farm labour contractor

(a) Wage rates

The contractor must post a notice at the site (usually a farm) where the work is performed which clearly states the wage rates. The notice must also be displayed on any vehicle which transports employees to the site.

A written statement showing the wages paid to each employee must be available for inspection by the employees. The purpose of the provisions concerning wages is to ensure that the employees are aware of exactly what monies should be paid to them, so that the contractor does not take advantage of the workers.

43

(b) Wages

Wages are paid according to the amount of crop picked. The rates below change frequently. They are accurate as of July 1, 1994.

(a) Raspberries — $0.235 per pound

(b) Strawberries — $0.225 per pound

(c) Blueberries — $0.295 per pound

(d) Cherries — $0.16 per pound

(e) Apples — $12.05 per bin (27.1 cubic feet)

(f) Pears — $13.56 per bin

(g) Apricots — $12.81 per ½ bin (13.7 cubic feet)

(h) Peaches — $12.81 per ½ bin

(i) Prunes — $13.56 per ½ bin

(j) Grapes — $12.81 per ½ bin (12.6 cubic feet)

(k) Brussel sprouts — $0.105 per pound

(l) Beans — $0.15 per pound

(m) Peas — $0.19 per pound

(n) Mushrooms $0.165 per pound

(c) Payment of wages

Wages must be paid not later than 72 hours after each pay period. A pay period is seven days. The contractor is required to pay each employee all wages earned at that time, with the exception of wages for the annual vacation. Failure to pay wages within this pay period is an offence under the act.

(d) Daily guaranteed minimum pay

Most farm labour contractors provide transportation to the work site. If, after transporting the employees, there is no work available, the contractor must pay a minimum amount to each employee. This pay is the greater of —

(a) four hours at the hourly minimum rate, or

(b) the hourly minimum rate for the time period from departure to return to the same place, or another place acceptable to the employee.

No minimum pay is necessary if work is unavailable because of poor weather or other reasons completely beyond the control of the farm labour contractor.

(e) Payroll list

The contractor must keep a current payroll list of all employees and provide it to the person who contracts for the farm labour services, upon request. Failure to provide such a list on demand is an offence under the act.

(f) Fee division

It is important that the farm labour contractor conduct business ethically. Fee inducements are prohibited. The contractor cannot give a fee or any other benefit to the person for whom the employees work. The contractor cannot accept any fee or benefit from the applicant or worker.

There is a special penalty for breaching this rule: a fine of up to $10 000 or imprisonment of up to six months, or both. This is the most serious penalty under the rules that govern farm labour contractors.

A farm labour contractor who violates any of the other rules can be fined up to $2 000.

c. APPRENTICES

Trades can be learned through the process of apprenticeship. A person, usually a young person, enters into an agreement with a skilled trades person to learn certain skills under his or her supervision. The trades person is called the principal. Upon completion of an apprenticeship period, the apprentice may take prescribed examinations in order to qualify for a certificate of apprenticeship.

The Apprenticeship Act regulates the training of apprentices. An apprenticeship board sets qualifications for entrance and certification in trades and oversees the system of apprenticeship in this province. The Director of Apprenticeship supervises the registration and certification requirements.

1. The apprenticeship agreement

An apprenticeship agreement is a contract between the apprentice and the principal. The apprenticeship board determines the terms and form of the agreement.

These agreements, unlike other contracts, can be entered into by a young person under the age of 19. The director can set the number of apprentices who can be employed by any single employer.

The act lists two types of trades: designated and apprenticeable. Apprenticeship agreements for a designated trade must be registered with the director to have effect. Apprenticeship agreements for apprenticeable trades can, with the consent of the principal and the apprentice, be registered with the director.

The director can cancel or refuse to register an apprenticeship agreement if he or she believes it would not be in the best interests of the apprentice. These agreements can be cancelled, assigned, or terminated by either party, the apprentice or the principal.

To assign the agreement means that the principal is replaced by another principal. The director must first approve the assignment and both parties must agree.

Where the agreement is registered with the director, the apprentice and principal must notify the director in writing of any of these changes. The director must determine what further training or experience is required for completion of the apprenticeship.

The duties of the director of apprenticeship include the following:

(a) The establishment of the registration and certification system

(b) The issuance of certificates of apprenticeship and of qualification

(c) The monitoring of the quality of apprenticeship training

(d) The development of course content and apprentice examinations

(e) The resolution of any question from the principal or apprentice about his or her rights and duties under the apprenticeship agreement

2. Types of trades

(a) Designated trades

Apprenticeship agreements for these trades must be registered with the director:

- Automotive body repair
- Automotive mechanical repair
- Automotive painting and refinishing
- Automotive parts warehousing and merchandising
- Automotive radiator manufacture and repair
- Automotive trimming
- Barbering
- Boilermaking
- Boilermaking (erection)
- Bookbinding
- Bricklaying
- Carpentry
- Cement masonry
- Commercial transport vehicle mechanical repair
- Cooking

- Domestic radio and television servicing
- Drywall finishing
- Electrical work
- Embalming
- Floor covering
- Glazing
- Hairdressing
- Heavy-duty mechanical repair
- Industrial instrumentation
- Ironworks
- Jewellery manufacture and repair
- Joinery (benchwork)
- Lithography
- Lumber manufacturing industry: benchman, circular sawfiler, construction millwright, sawfitter, steam and pipe fitting
- Machinist
- Millwright
- Moulding
- Office machine repair
- Oil burner repair
- Painting and decorating
- Pattern making
- Pile driving and bridgeman
- Plastering
- Plumbing
- Refrigeration
- Roofing, damp and waterproofing
- Servicing and repair of electrical appliances
- Sheet metal work

- Ship and boatbuilding
- Shipfitting
- Sign and pictorial painting
- Sprinkler fitting
- Steamfitting and pipefitting
- Steel fabrication
- Wall and ceiling installation
- Watch repair

(b) Compulsory certificates of qualification

The following designated trades require certificates of qualification before a person can practice or be employed in them:

- Plumbing
- Refrigeration
- Roofing, damp and waterproofing
- Sheet metal work
- Sprinkler fitting
- Steamfitting and pipefitting

The director can, in certain circumstances, grant an exemption from the requirement of a certificate.

(c) Apprenticeable trades

Apprenticeship agreements for these trades may be registered with the director:

- Aircraft maintenance
- Armature winder
- Baking
- Cableman
- Carman
- Cladding
- Dental mechanic
- Dental technician

- Diesel engine mechanical repair
- Electronics: audio and radio servicing, community antenna television, industrial, instrument repair and calibration, marine, panels and controls, radio communications, telecommunications
- Elevator mechanic
- Gas fitting
- Heat and frost insulating
- Inboard/ outboard mechanical repair
- Industrial warehousing
- Letter pressman
- Lineman
- Machinist-fitter
- Maintenance mechanic (pipeline industry)
- Marine engine mechanical repair
- Meat cutting
- Partsman
- Plastic and rubber fabrication
- Practical horticulture
- Power engineering
- Printer
- Small engine repair
- Tile setting
- Tire repair
- Tool and die making
- Welding

3

THE COMPLAINT PROCESS

It is the responsibility of all employers to comply with the standards for wages, working conditions, and benefits set out in the Employment Standards Act. An employee whose rights may have been violated by an employer can file a complaint with the Director of Employment Standards. (The regional offices of the Employment Standards Act are listed in the Appendix.) The most frequent complaint is that wages were not paid.

a. GENERAL

1. Who enforces the act?

The Director of Employment Standards oversees the enforcement of the act. Officers, who can be industrial relations officers or employment standards officers, investigate complaints, try to resolve the complaints, and make recommendations to the director.

These officers have a right of access to work premises, and to anywhere that employment records are retained, to investigate complaints. They can enter a ship, vessel, vehicle, aircraft, or other means of conveyance or transport, factory, workshop or land, or other place where —

(a) work is done, will be done, or was done by employees,

(b) an employer carries on business,

(c) a record required under the Employment Standards Act is kept, and

(d) a matter or thing, to which the act applies, is or was taking place.

2. Responsibilities of an employer

The definition of employer includes any person who has control or direction of, or responsibility for, the employment of an employee. Every employer must keep certain records, in English, for each employee for a period of one year after they cease employment. The records must state the following:

(a) The employee's name, occupation, date of birth, and home address

(b) Wages earned

(c) Wages paid

(d) Hours worked per day

(e) Deductions, such as unemployment insurance, by amount and purpose

(f) The date the employee began work

(g) The date of each annual vacation, the amount of vacation pay given, and the period of employment to which the vacation relates

(h) The amount paid in substitution for a general holiday on termination of employment

(i) The number of days accumulated for general holidays

(j) The amount of vacation pay given on termination of employment

The failure to keep these records can result in conviction under the act and a fine of up to $2 000. The records must be kept at the employer's principal place of business in British Columbia, unless the director allows the employer to keep the records at another place.

The purpose of requiring that such records be maintained is to allow investigators to inspect the records when a complaint is made. The records can be removed and copied by investigators. Upon demand, the employer must produce the records and may be required to deliver them to the investigators.

It is also an offence for an employer to knowingly make a false or misleading statement, or give false or misleading information concerning an employee's records.

b. THE COMPLAINT PROCESS

1. Time of the complaint

A complaint must be made within six months after the subject matter of the complaint occurs. If the complaint is about an employer's failure to pay wages, it must be made within six months of the last date wages were paid.

The person making the complaint is called the complainant. The employer is called the respondent.

2. Protection of the complainant

Two rules protect the rights of a person to complain:

(a) The complainant can ask that his or her identity be kept confidential.

(b) An employer who takes any disciplinary action against a complainant can be convicted of an offence under the act.

(a) Confidentiality

The act protects the identity of a complainant who requests confidentiality. Often an employee wants a complaint to remain confidential in order to protect his or her employment. Where the complainant asks in writing that his or her name and identity be confidential, it cannot be disclosed. The only exception is when disclosure is required for the purposes of a proceeding under the act, or disclosure is necessary in the public interest.

Information obtained by the director or his or her officers is also confidential. No person may inspect the information, with the exception of the Ombudsman. The Ombudsman acts in the public interest.

Unless there is a court prosecution, the director or his or her officers are not required to give evidence or produce records of any information obtained during an investigation under the act.

(b) Penalty for violation of the right to make a complaint

Section 58 of the act prohibits an employer's improper treatment of an employee who initiates a complaint or gives information to the director or officers:

An employer shall not

(a) terminate or threaten to terminate an employee,

(b) discipline or suspend an employee,

(c) impose a penalty on an employee, or

(d) intimidate or coerce an employee because of an investigation or action that may be or has been taken under the act or because the employee

(e) has registered a complaint under this act, or

(f) has supplied or may supply information to the director or his or her authorized representative.

The possible orders that can be made against an employer who violates this section include:

(a) An order to cease doing the act in question

(b) An order to reinstate a terminated employee

(c) An order to repay wages lost because of a wrongful termination

(d) An order to pay compensation to a terminated employee

3. The investigation process

The officer first investigates the complaint to determine whether it is valid. All complaints made within the six-month time limit must be investigated, with the following exceptions:

(a) Any complaint where the person or employee has pursued and received other legal remedies for the subject of the complaint

(b) Any complaint that is found to be frivolous, vexatious, trivial, or initiated in bad faith

(c) Any complaint not supported by sufficient evidence

No complaints will be investigated where the employee or person has commenced a civil action to recover money owed in the courts.

Once the officer determines there is a valid complaint, the next step is to try to resolve the issue and obtain compliance with the act. For example, if the complaint concerns unpaid wages, the officer will meet with the employer and try to persuade the employer to pay the necessary money owing to the employee.

The officer can issue an order requiring the money to be paid immediately to the director. The order must be served on the person, usually the employer. Registered mail is sufficient means of serving the person.

If the order is not paid, the officer will refer the complaint to the director for a further review. The director has one important power where the complaint concerns unpaid wages: a certificate can be issued against the employer that sets out the wages owing to an employee or person.

The director or an officer can investigate without receiving a complaint from an employee where it is necessary to determine whether an employer is complying with the act.

c. HOW TO RECOVER UNPAID WAGES

1. Remedies

The most common complaint against an employer is failure to pay wages. There are several mechanisms for recovery of money owed:

(a) A civil action for breach of the employment contract can be commenced in small claims court where the amount is $10 000 or less, or in Supreme Court if the amount is more than $10 000. This action is a personal action and no assistance is available from the Director of Employment Standards.

(b) The officer reaches a settlement with the employer, who agrees to pay the money to the employee or to the officer to be paid to the employee.

(c) Where no settlement is reached, an order in writing requiring payment to the director can be issued against the employer.

2. Employment Standards Act collection procedures

Officers are available to assist employees who are owed unpaid wages or other money under the act. A complaint for payment of unpaid wages must be made within the six-month time limit.

There are two steps in the collection process under the act. The first step is to obtain an order from an officer for payment of the money. The order demands that the money be paid to the director. The person against whom the order is made can ask the director to review the order.

Once the order is issued against an employer, the complainant cannot begin any other proceedings, such as civil proceedings, without the written consent of the director.

Employers must be notified in the order for payment of their right to review. The employer may have valid reasons for not paying the wages and that decision is entitled to a review by the director.

The request for a review of the order of payment must —

(a) be in writing,

(b) be made within eight days of receipt of the order, or longer time period, with the consent of the director,

(c) include reasons for seeking a review, and

(d) include a certified cheque or money order, payable to the director, for $100 or 10% of the amount owing, whichever is greater, as a deposit.

The director, when reviewing the order, may hold an actual hearing, although this is not mandatory. Further information may be requested from the employer or the employee. On completion of the review, the director must confirm, vary, or cancel the order. The deposit money is returned to the employer, should the director cancel the order.

Where the employer has not requested a review of the officer's order for unpaid wages, or where the director has, after a review, confirmed or varied that order, the next step is the issuance of a certificate. The director issues the certificate against the employer, which states the amount of money owing. This certificate permits the government to forfeit the deposit as a fee for the unsuccessful review. The certificate is then filed in court and has the same effect as a court judgment. The employee who is owed the money pays no legal costs for this procedure.

The employer may file an appeal of the director's certificate in the Supreme Court. Any appeal must be filed within 45 days of the decision. A trial will be held, and again, the employee does not pay any legal costs because the director defends the action on behalf of the employee.

3. Enforcement

There are several ways of collecting the unpaid wages and the director chooses which will be the most effective, depending on the circumstances of the employer or person whoowes the debt. The money recovered is then paid to the complainant.

The certificate is a secured debt in favour of the director. This means that it is like a charge against all real or personal property of the person owing the money. ("Real property" is the legal term for land, while "personal property" includes possessions of value such as cars and boats.)

Sometimes the employer does not have sufficient money or property to pay his or her debts. The issue is then which debts have priority. The certificate has priority over other debts of the employer, with the exception of a mortgage registered against the real property of the employer, filed before the certificate is issued.

(a) Seizure of assets

Any assets owned or possessed by the person owing the money can be seized and sold. They are kept by the sheriff, who is responsible for seizing the assets until the order is cancelled, or the certificate is filed in court. The sheriff can then sell the seized goods.

Costs of the seizure are paid to the director, as well as the amount of money stated on the certificate. The director then pays the unpaid wages to the employee or person, according to the process described under subsection **(e)** below.

Only the director or his or her representative, such as a sheriff, can seize assets from the person who owes wages.

(b) Demand for money from a third party

A demand for payment can be issued against several third parties, including banks, credit unions, trust companies, and individuals who owe money to the debtor/employer. For example, if a certificate for unpaid wages is issued against an employer, and the employer has money in a bank account, the director can issue a demand for the money against that bank.

The third party must pay the money to the director within 15 days of service of the demand, or when the money was owed.

(c) Liability of directors and officers of corporations

Many places of employment are incorporated businesses. This means that the corporation is actually the legal employer. To recover money owed for wages to an employee, special rules make directors or officers of the corporation personally liable for unpaid wages and severance pay.

Directors or officers can be required to pay up to two months' unpaid wages owed to each employee. The director can issue a certificate against the director or officer and recover the money using the normal collection procedures.

If the corporation cannot pay its debts and is in receivership or is bankrupt, the directors and officers are not liable for severance pay.

A director or officer of a registered charity is not personally liable for unpaid wages, but other directors or officers are liable. They can be required to pay up to two months' unpaid wages owed to each employee.

(d) Liability of associated corporations

To protect creditors, such as employees owed unpaid wages, where several corporations are essentially under common control or direction, the director can recover payment under the certificate from these corporations.

(e) Distribution of money paid to the director

Money recovered by the director under the certificate is held in trust by the Minister of Finance. Often an employer owes money to more than one employee. The director tries to recover enough money to pay all the employees. If not, the money collected is paid proportionately to the employees.

For example, if six employees are owed $1 000 each and the director recovers $3 000 from the employer, each employee is paid $500.

4. Collection in the courts

An employee can choose not to use the enforcement procedures under the Employment Standards Act, but to sue the employer directly in court for breach of contract for the unpaid wages.

A lawsuit can be conducted through small claims court, which hears claims for debts of $10 000 or less. The small claims court follows a less formal structure than the higher courts, and people can use it to resolve disputes fairly, quickly, and cheaply. It is not necessary to hire a lawyer.

Information about the rules and forms used in small claims court can be obtained from any provincial court registry. This material is written in plain language and designed to assist the non-lawyer. A further source of information about small claims court procedure is the Self-Counsel publication, *Small Claims Court Guide for British Columbia.*

Once judgment is won against the employer, there are several ways to collect the money. For example, if the employer owns personal assets, they can be seized and sold (see section **3. (a)** above). Alternatively, if the employer has a bank account or receives wages, garnishment may be effective.

Garnishment is the process by which a third party is ordered to pay money owed to the debtor into court. Garnishment rules are complex and included in the Court Order Enforcement Act. The small claims court has forms to use that explain how to garnish wages or a bank account in a step-by-step process.

A certain amount of a persons's wages are exempt from garnishment, generally 70%. The purpose is to ensure that the debtor has enough money to support himself or herself and any dependants.

5. Deceased workers' wages

When a worker dies, the wages earned by the deceased worker during the three months prior to his or her death, and any other money owed, such as holiday pay, are paid directly to the widow or widower. Widows and widowers do not have to wait until the estate of the deceased spouse is distributed.

No other surviving relative qualifies for these wages. If there is no surviving spouse, the money does not need to be paid immediately.

To make a claim for these wages, the widower or widow must give an affidavit to the employer stating that he or she is the widower or widow. (An affidavit is a statement sworn before a notary public or lawyer.)

A common-law spouse who was living with the deceased worker for two years prior to his or her death, and was supported by the deceased during this period, is also eligible for this benefit.

4

HUMAN RIGHTS PROTECTIONS

The B.C. Human Rights Act governs provincial human rights issues. The purpose of human rights legislation is to ensure that people are treated on the basis of individual characteristics and abilities, not on the basis of any presumed or actual group characteristics. The B.C. Council of Human Rights receives, investigates, and resolves complaints of discrimination.

Whenever possible, a complaint is resolved through mediation and agreement of the parties. In other cases, a hearing is held where the complainant and the alleged discriminator can each state their side of the case. Several remedies are available, including compensation for lost wages, reinstatement to a job, and money to compensate for injuries to self-respect or hurt feelings.

The majority of complaints received by the council relate to discrimination in employment. Sex discrimination, including sexual harassment and discrimination because of pregnancy, is the leading complaint, followed by physical disability.

Discrimination in the workplace includes many forms of conduct, from refusing to hire a person because of his or her race to different rates of pay to male and female employees for similar work.

Employers must be sensitive to the issues discussed in this chapter. They should also be aware that they are liable for the discriminatory practices of their employees.

The Supreme Court of Canada recently added a requirement to provincial human rights rules to ensure that every worker can fully participate in the workplace. The court said that employers have a duty to accommodate the individual needs of employees in order to encourage equality of opportunity in employment.

Employers should, where possible, modify work rules or practices to meet the needs of individuals or groups, such as pregnant women or people with disabilities. The employer is excused from the duty to accommodate when it would cause undue hardship.

However, often all that is required is that an employer provide a flexible work schedule or adaptive technology designed for people with physical disabilities, for example.

a. GROUNDS OF DISCRIMINATION

Discrimination is prohibited at every stage in the employment process, from the job interview to promotion rights on the job.

1. Discrimination in employment advertisements

An employer cannot advertise a potential job with certain limitations or preferences.

Section 6 of the act states:

> No person shall publish or cause to be published an advertisement in connection with employment or prospective employment that expresses a limitation, specification, or preference as to race, colour, ancestry, place of origin, political belief, religion, marital status, family status, physical or mental disability, sex, sexual orientation, or age unless the limitation, specification, or preference is based on a bona fide occupational requirement.

The procedure for filing a complaint concerning a discriminatory employment advertisement is the same procedure used to file a complaint for discrimination in employment (see **3.** below).

2. Discrimination in wages

An employer cannot pay different wages to male and female employees for similar work. However, if the difference in the rate of pay between employees of different sexes is based on a factor *other* than sex, then it does not constitute a failure to comply with the law.

In order to comply with this regulation, an employer must not reduce the rate of pay of the higher-paid employee.

For a complaint to be successful, an employee must prove the following:

(a) Different wage rates are paid for work that is similar or substantially similar.

(b) These different wages are paid to male and female employees.

(c) One sex of employee was paid lower wages than the other.

The factors used to determine whether two jobs are similar or substantially similar are the skill, effort, and responsibility required by each job. Skill means the experience, training, education, and ability required for the job. Effort means the quality and quantity of physical or mental exertion required for the job. Responsibility means the importance of the job and the degree of accountability required in performance of the job, including supervision of other employees and financial or health and safety supervisory tasks.

Where an employee can show that there is a difference in the rate of pay based on sex, he or she can recover the difference between the wages paid, and the wages paid to the other employee in the same job.

An action to recover wage differences can commence either while an employee is employed, or after he or she has left employment. However, there are some limits to the action:

(a) The action must begin within 12 months of termination of the employment if the employee is terminated.

(b) Only 12 months' wage differences will be paid or awarded.

The hearing procedure is the same as for an action concerning discrimination in employment (see below).

3. Discrimination in employment or application for employment

Under the act, employers may not discriminate against an employee on the basis of race, colour, ancestry, place of origin, political belief, religion, marital status, family status, physical or mental disability, sex, sexual orientation, age, or because that person has been convicted of a criminal or summary conviction charge that is unrelated to the employment.

The prohibition against discrimination also applies to trade unions, employers' organizations, or occupational associations.

(a) Age

Employers cannot discriminate because of age where the job applicant or employee is between 19 and 64 years of age. Discrimination on the basis of age does not include plans or benefit programs that favour one age group over another. Section 8(3) of the act states that the prohibition against discrimination does not apply, as it relates to age, to schemes based on seniority.

Example:

The complainant, a 46-year-old man, applied for a position as a shipper/receiver, and was told that he was too old for the position. The employer argued that the job was suitable for younger men because it involved "dirty work," and that older men hired previously for the position did not stay in the job. The employer said he did not intend to discriminate.

The council held that the employer did discriminate and ordered that the complainant be paid damages for the loss of opportunity to compete for the position, and for the injury to his dignity and feelings of self-respect.

(b) Criminal convictions

Employers may attempt to question job applicants or employees about any criminal record or conviction. However, criminal convictions can be considered only if they are related to the employment. The length of time between the conviction and the employment, the nature of the conviction, and its severity and circumstances are factors to consider when determining whether a conviction relates to the employment in question.

Example:

The council considered a complaint on this ground in 1991, when a driver for a mobile catering company was fired after voluntarily telling the employer of a criminal conviction. The council found that the conviction did not concern either fraud or theft, and was unrelated to her employment. She was awarded damages.

(c) Sexual discrimination

Discrimination on the basis of sex takes many forms, including the following:

(a) Refusal to promote qualified women

(b) Refusal to employ or to continue to employ a pregnant woman

(c) The creation of job requirements that exclude women on the basis of their physical characteristics

(d) Sexual harassment of female employees by other male employees, or by the employer

Examples:

In 1994, the council awarded damages to a female drummer who was hired and then dismissed from a musical performance. She was dismissed because the producer wanted an all-male musical trio, since the show involved the vocalist flirting with the band. The council held that sex discrimination occurred, and that while gender may be relevant to some musical performances, the producer in this case should have altered the performance so that the female drummer would not be dismissed.

In another decision, a complainant who cut and wrapped vegetables for a produce market was fired when she became pregnant. The council found that this was discrimination on the basis of sex. It found that the complainant's pregnancy did not affect her ability to perform her job.

Sexual harassment is a particular form of sexual discrimination. The Supreme Court of Canada defined sexual harassment in the workplace in 1989 as "unwelcome conduct that detrimentally affects the work environment and leads to adverse job-related consequences for the victims of the harassment."

Employers should understand that they have a duty to provide a healthy work environment for every employee. Employers are responsible for the acts of employees who harass other employees. It is in their interest to ensure that all employees understand that any form of sexual harassment is prohibited in the workplace. Therefore, it is helpful for an employer to establish a policy concerning sexual harassment, what it is, and why it cannot occur in a workplace.

Sexual harassment is not defined in the act. It includes many forms of sexually oriented conduct, both verbal and physical, such as —

    (a) Nude photographs displayed in the workplace, for example on a calendar

(b) Unwanted touching

(c) Offensive comments concerning men or women

(d) Persistent propositions including requests for dates

(e) Blatant sexual comments

(d) Sexual orientation

Sexual orientation was added to the prohibited grounds of discrimination under the act in 1992, but is not yet the subject of any decisions of the council or the B.C. courts. However, other provinces have previously legislated sexual orientation as a ground of discrimination. The most common form of discrimination on this basis is a complaint that an employee's same sex partner is denied benefits that are available to a partner of the opposite sex, such as spousal medical benefits.

A court in another province found that such a denial was not discrimination on the basis of sexual orientation, but that the complainant was denied benefits because of his non-spousal status. However, a different court concluded that an employee benefits plan that denied a homosexual employee benefits for his same sex partner was discriminatory.

The issue of denial of benefits to same sex conjugal couples is still unresolved, and at the time of writing, it has not been determined in B.C.

(e) Religion

The religious beliefs of employees may require an employer to make certain accommodations, particularly in terms of scheduling work shifts to permit employees to honour religious holidays.

Example:

In a 1994 decision of the council, a complainant who worked as a mechanic for an agricultural firm was fired because he refused to work after sundown on Friday. Saturday was a holy day in his religion. The council found that the employer discriminated against the employee and did not take reasonable steps, short of undue hardship to the employer, to accommodate his religious beliefs.

The Supreme Court of Canada considered the same issue in 1994, when a union employee complained of discrimination on the basis of religion. Both the employer and the trade union were found to have discriminated against the employee. He was a school custodian whose religious beliefs prevented him from working from sundown Friday until sundown Sunday. While the employer, a school board, was prepared to schedule a special shift to accommodate his beliefs, the union did not agree. The employee was fired.

The court held that both employer and union had failed in their duty to reasonably accommodate the employee's religious beliefs.

(f) Physical or mental disability

What constitutes a physical or mental disability is not defined in the act. A chronic disease such as cancer or AIDS may be a physical disability if it makes specific types of employment difficult to perform or if it results in the employee's dismissal. Physical differences, such as obesity, may be considered a disability.

Example:

Height can be a physical disability if it is the basis of discrimination in employment. The council considered a complaint from an applicant for a job in a clothing store. She was 4'9" tall. Her initial interview was positive, but she was then told by the employer that she was not hired for the position because she was too short. She was not given an opportunity to show how high she could reach. The council awarded the complainant money for lost wages and money as compensation for humiliation.

The council has guidelines for employers concerning the employment of people with disabilities. These guidelines state that employing persons with disabilities may require modifications to the job or the work facilities. For example, an employer can consider flexible work schedules, physical alteration of certain facilities, and the acquisition of technical aids to assist an employee with disabilities.

(g) Marital status

Complaints of discrimination concerning marital status include cases where the complainant was treated in a discriminatory manner because of his or her spouse's criminal record, or job requirements preventing two married persons from working in the same workplace.

Unmarried marital status was recently the source of a complaint of discrimination.

Example:

An apartment building was managed by a single female employee. New owners purchased the building and fired the manager. The termination letter stated that the employer was of the opinion that a married couple would be more appropriate as managers.

The tenants of the building testified that the complainant was an excellent building manager. Her complaint was successful and the employer was ordered to cease from committing any similar violations, to pay her moving expenses, and to pay damages for lost wages, hurt feelings, and humiliation.

4. Intentional and unintentional discrimination

Discrimination can be intentional, or simply the unintentional result of a neutral employment policy that results in the favouring of one group over another. An example of direct discrimination is a restaurant's hiring policy that excludes all persons over the age of 45. This is direct discrimination on the basis of age.

An example of unintentional discrimination would be a hiring policy that requires all applicants to weigh 75 kilograms and stand 188 centimetres in height. This policy would exclude most female applicants and some male applicants. The employer may have no intention of excluding any category of persons, but it is the effect, not the purpose, of the policy that constitutes discrimination.

Recent court decisions have considered what constitutes unintentional discrimination. The Supreme Court of Canada heard a case in which the employer's work schedules required employees to work Saturdays. For some employees, including the complainant, Saturday was a day of religious observance. While the employer in this case had no intention to discriminate on the grounds of religion, the court found that there was an unintended adverse effect on certain employees because of the work schedule. Ordinary business practices may constitute discrimination.

5. Exceptions

Not all discriminatory employment practices are prohibited. Discrimination may be permitted in the following situations:

(a) A bona fide occupational requirement exists

(b) The employer is a charitable, philanthropic, educational, fraternal, religious, or social organization or corporation

(c) An employment equity program exists

(d) The ground of discrimination is age and there is a valid seniority scheme

(e) The ground of discrimination is sex, age, marital status, and physical or mental disability, and there is a bona fide retirement, superannuation, or pension plan or group or employee insurance plan

(f) The discrimination does not fall directly into one of the prohibited grounds, yet has an adverse effect on an employee, and the employer has made reasonable efforts to accommodate the employee

The defence most often used by an employer when a job applicant or employee complains of discrimination is that the job requirement in question was valid and made in good faith. This is called a bona fide occupational requirement.

The test for the defence of a bona fide occupational requirement is —

(a) the requirement is imposed honestly and in good faith, and

(b) the requirement is rationally connected to a valid business purpose that assures the efficient and economical performance of the job.

Example:

The ability to communicate in English may be a bona fide occupational requirement on a job site. In a 1991 B.C. Supreme Court case, the complainant argued discrimination because an employer who operated a sawmill refused to hire the complainant because of his poor English skills. The court held that there was no discrimination, and that the ability to communicate was necessary in the sawmill operation.

Employment equity programs are another exception to the discrimination rules. Employment equity programs are structured to provide disadvantaged groups or individuals with the opportunity of achieving equality in the workplace. It is permissible for an employer to give preference to members of a disadvantaged group, such as women or members of visible minorities.

b. THE COMPLAINT PROCESS

1. Filing a complaint

It is important that everyone feels free to make complaints concerning human rights violations, without fear of consequences.

The act states that no person may impose any penalty or discriminate against a person who makes a complaint. The possible penalty for violating this protection is a fine of up to $2 000, or imprisonment of up to six months, or both.

The person making the complaint is called the *complainant*. The person against whom the complaint is made is called the *respondent*. While the complainant is most often the actual subject of the alleged discrimination, another person or group may lay a complaint on behalf of a person or group of persons.

All enquiries concerning discrimination in employment are screened by human rights officers. They review the enquiry to see if it discloses a ground of discrimination prohibited by the act against a person or company. If so, the complainant then files a signed complaint form.

The complaint should identify the complainant and give specific details of the alleged discriminatory act. It is helpful to include the section of the Employment Standards Act that applies to the situation. The time and place of the conduct in question should be described with as much accuracy as possible.

The chair of the council, or another member of the council, reviews the complaint to decide whether it should be investigated. The council can dismiss the following types of complaints without investigation.

(a) Complaints not within the jurisdiction of the council, for example, complaints directed against a federal, not provincial, employer

(b) Complaints found after preliminary investigation to be trivial, frivolous, vexatious, or made in bad faith

(c) Complaints based on facts that occurred more than six months prior to the filing of the complaint (However, if the delay was a result of good faith on the part of the complainant and no substantial prejudice will result to anyone, the complaint can be investigated.)

If there is a decision not to investigate the complaint, the complainant must be informed in writing. If there is a decision to investigate the complaint, the respondent is served with a copy. This gives the respondent an opportunity to understand the allegations and to prepare a response. The employer-respondent may choose to hire a lawyer who can be present at any hearing or at any meetings with the complainant or investigator.

2. The investigation process

Once a complaint reaches the investigation stage, it is assigned to an officer in the Employment Standards Branch. (Offices of the Employment Standards Branch are listed in the Appendix.)

Investigators conduct interviews with each party and any witnesses and collect any records or documents relating to the complaint. They attempt to mediate the issue and they prepare a report summarizing the investigation for the council.

The council attempts, wherever possible, to mediate complaints of discrimination. Mediation is the process of bringing the parties together to settle their differences without a hearing. Both parties must agree to any terms of settlement offered through mediation.

Successful mediation offers a positive outcome to both parties. The time and expense of a hearing is avoided, and matters can be resolved quickly. Often, an employer will, after mediation, agree to reinstate a complainant terminated for discriminatory reasons, or compensate him or her for damages suffered.

If mediation is not successful, or if the parties do not want to mediate the complaint, the officer prepares the investigation report, which is sent to both the complainant and the respondent. Each party has 30 days to respond to the report. If the responses reveal new information, this is disclosed to the other party.

Disclosure is important, because each party must understand the issues to be argued at the hearing. Disclosure can also encourage settlement, which can occur at any stage of the process. For example, if the report clearly concludes that an employer has discriminated against a job applicant on the basis of age, it may encourage the employer to settle the complaint without a hearing.

c. THE HEARING

The council, after considering the investigator's report, can decide to:

(a) discontinue the complaint on the grounds that there is no reasonable basis for a hearing,

(b) report to the Minister, or

(c) hold a hearing.

Hearings to determine whether an employer has discriminated against a job applicant or employee are held before a single member of the human rights council. All hearings are open to the public. Each side presents their argument to the member of council hearing the matter. The council member can give a decision orally or in writing.

A complaint will be dismissed if it is found at the hearing to be unjustifiable or unacceptable, in which case a remedy will be ordered.

d. REMEDIES

Where a board of inquiry determines that a complaint of discrimination in employment is proven, the respondent can be ordered to pay financial compensation to the complainant. There is no upper limit to the amount of the award, but damages have not yet exceeded $5 000.

The amount is based on the injury to dignity, feelings, and self-respect of the complainant. The council considers all the circumstances of the discrimination, including the time period, the attitude and conduct of the person who discriminates, the age and vulnerability of the victim, and any other factor that affects the impact on the complainant.

Other remedies include the following:

(a) A cease and desist order which tells the employer to stop the prohibited conduct

(b) A declaration that the conduct in question is discriminatory

(c) Reinstatement of an employee who was terminated from employment

(d) Lost wages, where an employee has lost his or her job

5

WORKERS' COMPENSATION

Workers who suffer work-related disease, injury, or death are entitled to financial compensation under the Workers' Compensation Act. A worker must establish a causal relationship between the work activities and a diagnosed injury or disease. All workers in B.C. are protected by the act, with the exception of those employers or workers exempted by order of the board.

The compensation scheme is similar to no-fault insurance: where the worker contributes, through negligence, to the injury, he or she may still receive benefits. The only exception is where an injury is the sole result of a worker's serious and willful misconduct. No compensation is payable in those circumstances unless the injury results in death or serious or permanent disablement.

Two types of basic compensation are available: wage loss benefits for a temporary injury or occupational disease, and a pension, where the injury or disease is permanent.

Rehabilitation services are also available to injured workers, and may include job re-training. The purpose of these services is to return the worker to the work force, wherever possible.

The act is administered by the Workers' Compensation Board. The board is responsible for approving and implementing policies concerning compensation of workers, assessment of employers' payments, rehabilitation of workers, and definition of occupational health and safety standards.

The board consists of 13 governors: five represent workers, five represent employers, two represent the public interest, and one is the chair. This board also administers other regulations that affect safety in the workplace, including the industrial health and safety regulations, the first aid regulations, the workplace hazardous information system regulations, and the occupational environmental regulations.

Compensation is paid to workers from the accident fund, which is funded entirely by employer contributions. The board assesses the amount of each employer's contribution to the accident fund. This assessment reflects the potential health and safety risks of the workplace.

It is unlawful for an employer to directly or indirectly deduct any money for the accident fund from the wages of an employee. Should an employer deduct money for this purpose, he or she must repay the worker the full amount of the deductions.

a. PERSONAL INJURY

Most claims by workers for compensation are for injuries that arise "out of or in the course of employment." This definition is found in the act and gives the board broad powers to consider many different factors in determining what is an employment-related injury. The board must consider the folowing questions about each claim for injury:

- (a) Did the injury occur on the employer's premises?

- (b) Did the injury occur while the employee was doing something of benefit to the employer?

- (c) Did the injury occur during an activity of the employee done in response to the employer's instructions?

- (d) Did the injury occur while the employee was using equipment or materials supplied by the employer?

- (e) Did the injury occur while the employee was receiving payment or other consideration from the employer?

(f) Was the injury caused by some activity of the employer or another employee?

Accidents that occur in the course of travel from a worker's home to the place of employment are not employment related, unless the worker is employed to travel. A worker does not cease to be in the course of employment during a meal break or coffee break if these are taken on the employer's premises. For example, if a worker slips and falls in the lunchroom, the injuries will be considered to be work related, even though at the time the worker was not actually working.

Psychological impairment as well as physical injury is recognized as personal injury. For example, a worker may be disabled due to post-traumatic stress disorder.

A worker may suffer an injury that worsens a pre-existing disability. Compensation is paid only for the proportion of the disability that follows the personal injury.

b. OCCUPATIONAL DISEASE

An occupational disease is defined as a disease due to the nature of any employment in which the worker was employed. The issue is always one of causation: was the disease caused by work activities of the employee? If the disease keeps the worker from earning full wages, or causes his or her death, compensation is payable.

A list of recognized occupational diseases is found in Schedule "B" of the act. There must be scientific evidence of a causal relation between the disease and the nature of the employment before the board can designate a disease as an occupational disease. If a worker suffers from a disease listed in this schedule, and works in the occupation that contributes to the disease, there is a presumption that the disease was work related. A worker's occupation may also worsen a pre-existing disease. The worker will receive compensation for the proportion of disability following the disease.

Examples of occupational disease include the following:

(a) Silicosis, where the worker is exposed to silica dust as a coal miner

(b) Heart injury or disease, where the worker is a fire fighter

(c) Tendinitis, where the employment requires unaccustomed and repetitive use of the affected hand, arm, leg, or foot

(d) Lung cancer, where there is prolonged exposure to the dust of uranium

(e) Lead poisoning, where there is exposure to lead or lead compounds

These are only some examples of diseases linked scientifically to certain occupations for which workers can receive compensation.

A worker may suffer from a disease not yet recognized as an occupational disease, yet believe that it was caused by his or her employment. Workers must establish that their disease is an occupational disease and that it probably resulted from work activities. It may be more difficult to show that a disease is work related than an injury because of the different possible causes of many diseases and the length of time they may take to develop.

c. BENEFITS

Workers' compensation benefits include —

(a) wage loss benefits, paid where the injury or disease is temporary,

(b) a pension, paid where the injury or disease is permanent, or

(c) rehabilitation and job retraining services.

1. Benefit amounts

The amount of benefits paid changes twice a year, on January 1 and July 1, to reflect changes in the consumer price index. As of July 1, 1994, the following rates of compensation are accurate.

(a) Permanent total disability: Workers who suffer a permanent total disability that prevents them from any future employment due to injury or disease, receive compensation for life equal to 75% of their average earnings. The compensation must not be less than $1 147.99 per month.

(b) Permanent partial disability: Workers who suffer a permanent but partial disability receive payment equal to 75% of the estimated loss of their future earning capacity. Payments can be made in one lump sum or periodically for life. A rating schedule of percentages of impairment of earning capacity for specified injuries is used as a guide in determining the appropriate amount of compensation. Workers who suffer a permanent partial disability may also receive other benefits, such as occupational retraining.

(c) Permanent partial disfigurement: Workers who suffer a permanent and serious disfigurement that impairs future earning capacity may receive compensation payable on the same terms as a permanent partial disability.

(d) Temporary disability: Workers who suffer a temporary disability, either total or partial, receive wage loss benefits. A temporary injury is an injury that, in the opinion of the Workers' Compensation Board doctor, will get better in less than 12 months. If the injury becomes permanent, wage loss benefits are not paid. The worker must apply for a pension instead of wage loss benefits.

Where the temporary disability is total, the compensation equals 75% of the worker's average earnings. It must not be less than $264.90 per week.

Where the temporary disability is partial, the compensation equals 75% of the difference between the worker's average earnings before the injury, and the average amount the worker earns, or could earn, in some suitable employment after the injury.

A review of the amount of money a temporarily injured worker will receive on a long-term basis is held after eight weeks of wage loss payments. The issue to determine is the amount of the injured worker's "average earnings."

(e) Death: Several benefits are payable when a worker dies due to injury or occupational disease.

    (i) Funeral expenses of $2 119.19 and incidental expenses related to the death of the worker of up to $706.41 will be paid by the accident fund. The employer is liable for the cost of transporting the deceased worker's body, where the death occurs on the job, to the nearest undertaker's place of business. Should burial not take place there, the accident fund pays up to $706.41 for the cost of additional transportation.

    (ii) A pension can be paid to certain beneficiaries of the deceased worker. The amount of payment varies, according to the average earnings of the deceased worker, the age of the widow or widower, the existence of dependent children, the number of dependent children, and whether the surviving spouse is entitled to government pension benefits.

(iii) The definition of spouse includes both married persons and a common-law wife or husband. Where the deceased worker lived with and contributed to the support and maintenance of a common-law spouse with whom he or she had no children for three or more years, the common-law spouse receives all the benefits of a widow or widower. Where the couple had children and lived together for one or more years, the surviving spouse is a common-law spouse within the act and receives all the benefits of a widow or widower.

(iv) Where the dependant is a widow or widower, who, at the date of the death of the worker, is 50 years of age or over, or is an invalid, the monthly payments cannot be less than $741.61. Where the dependant is a widow or widower who is under the age of 40, not an invalid, and there are no dependent children, a capital sum of $35 320.60 is payable. It must be paid within six months of the date of the death of the worker, unless the dependant asks the board to delay payment. Where the dependant is a widow or widower who is between the ages of 40 and 49, not an invalid, and there are no dependent children, he or she receives a monthly payment of no less than $741.61.

(v) Where a deceased worker leaves both a common-law spouse and a dependent widow or widower, the board may divide the benefits between the two.

(vi) Where the worker and dependent spouse were living separate and apart at the time of the worker's death, payment of any benefits depends upon the date of the separation and whether there is a separation agreement or court order for support payments. Where there was no support order and the couple lived separate and apart for less than three months prior to the date of death of the worker, the compensation will be the same as if the couple lived together at the time of death. Where the couple lived apart for three months or more, the board will give payments equal to the amount of support likely to have been paid by the deceased worker.

(vii) Monthly payments awarded by the board to a dependent spouse are payable for the lifetime of that spouse unless he or she remarries or lives in a common-law relationship. In such cases, he or she is entitled to a sum equal to payments for two years.

2. Average earnings

A worker's "average earnings" are assessed in order to determine the amount of wage loss benefits or the pension. Many factors are examined in order to reach a figure which fairly reflects these average earnings, including —

(a) the worker's daily, weekly, or monthly wages, or

(b) the worker's average yearly wages for one or more years prior to the date of the compensation claim, or

(c) the probable future earning capacity of the worker, or

(d) the average rate for the worker's occupation.

Where the worker's earnings do not accurately reflect average earnings or probable future earnings, the board can consider the probable future increase in the "average earnings" the worker would have earned, if he or she had not been injured. This is important where the worker has recently entered the work force, or where the worker is injured while learning a trade or occupation.

3. Annual adjustment of compensation

Each award of compensation that is paid periodically is adjusted every year to reflect the changes in the cost of living.

4. Claims against the compensation

By law, the money received as compensation under the act is not taxable. As well, this money cannot be attached by a creditor to pay for a debt owed by the worker, nor can it be assigned to a third person by the worker.

5. Discontinuance of payments

Payments can be discontinued or suspended in several circumstances:

(a) Where a worker is imprisoned, the compensation can be withheld, suspended, or paid to the worker's spouse or children.

(b) Where a worker is not supporting his or her spouse or children who are in need, the compensation can be paid to the spouse or children.

(c) Where there is an unpaid support order for the benefit of the worker's spouse or children, the compensation can be paid to the spouse or children.

Payments can be reduced or suspended where a worker —

(a) persists in unsanitary or injurious practices that delay his or her recovery, or

(b) refuses to undergo medical or surgical treatment that the board considers, based on expert medical advice, reasonably essential to the worker's recovery.

6. Rehabilitation benefits

If a work-related injury or disease prevents a worker from returning to his or her old job, rehabilitation and retraining benefits are available. These services include counselling, educational upgrading, retraining for the job, and job search assistance.

For example, a worker who suffers a serious back injury may be unable to return to work if the job involved heavy physical labour. Retraining for a new occupation may be the best assistance the board can offer the worker.

d. HOW TO CLAIM BENEFITS

Claims for compensation must be made under the act, and officers of the board determine the validity of the claim. A worker can receive assistance from the workers' advisers who operate independently of the board. Their role is to help workers at every stage of the claim for compensation.

An employer can receive assistance from the employers' advisers who also operate independently of the board. Their role is to help employers.

Applications for compensation must be in the form prescribed by the board, signed by the worker or his or her dependant, and made within one year of the injury, death, or disablement from occupational disease. However, there are exceptions to these rules. The board can pay compensation under the following circumstances:

(a) Without an application in special circumstances

(b) If special circumstances precluded filing the application within the one-year time limit (in which case, the application must be filed within three years)

(c) Where the application is a claim for an occupational disease, but there was no sufficient medical or scientific evidence available within one year from the date of the worker's death or disability that the disease was an occupational disease (The application must then be filed within three years from the date the disease is recognized by the board as an occupational disease.)

An injured worker must report any accident or occupational disease to the employer as soon as possible. If an accident occurs, the worker must include the names of any witnesses to the accident. The survivor of a deceased worker who died as a result of an accident or occupational disease should also report the death to the employer.

e. MEDICAL EXAMINATIONS

While some injuries or diseases are clearly work related, others may require further medical evidence of work related causation. The board can require a worker to attend a medical examination by a physician chosen by the board. The worker must cooperate or his or her right to receive compensation will be suspended until this examination takes place.

f. OTHER POWERS OF THE BOARD

The board and its officers play a fundamental role in the prevention of occupational injuries and diseases, as well as the investigation and payment of compensation. Employers should be aware of the board's many powers to regulate health and safety employment standards. These powers are enforced through fines and assessments against employers who do not comply with the health and safety standards. Money collected in fines or assessments is paid into the accident fund.

The board can —

(a) issue orders specifying requirements to be adopted in any place of employment for the prevention of injuries and occupational diseases, and

(b) inspect any place of employment to ensure that the employer is complying with health and safety standards.

An officer of the board has the power to investigate any accident that results in the injury or death of a worker and can inspect health and safety matters at any place of employment.

1. Penalties

To encourage employers to make the workplace as safe as possible, the board may order payment against an employer of additional assessments if it is determined that the place of employment is unsafe, or that the employer is not taking sufficient precautions to prevent injuries and occupational disease.

The employer can be fined up to $35 320.60 if, after investigation of a claim, the board considers the worker's injury, death, or disablement from disease was due substantially to —

(a) the gross negligence of the employer,

(b) the employer's failure to adopt reasonable means for the prevention of injuries or industrial diseases, or

(c) the employer's failure to comply with orders or directions of the board, or with certain regulations.

Finally, the board has the authority to close a place of employment if it considers that conditions of immediate danger exist that would likely result in serious injury, death, or occupational disease to workers. This order of closure must be confirmed in writing within 24 hours by the board or it will expire.

Failure to comply with a closure order is a serious offence. An employer who does not comply with the closure order commits an offence and is liable on conviction to a fine not exceeding $176 603.17, or to imprisonment not exceeding six months, or to both.

2. Agreement to waive compensation

A worker cannot agree with an employer to waive any benefits under the act. The act prohibits both employers and their supervisory employees from threatening or persuading a worker, or his or her dependants, by any means from reporting to the board an injury, industrial disease, death, or hazardous condition in any employment.

It is no defence for the employer to argue that the injury or other matter would not receive compensation under the act. Any decision about whether an injury, disease, or death is compensable under the act is made by the board or its officers, and not by an employer.

An employer who commits this offence can be fined up to $17 660.39. A worker with supervisory responsibilities who commits this offence can be fined up to $3 532.12.

g. APPEALS

A worker can appeal the medical decision of the board or any decision of a claims officer. There is a further right of appeal to the appeal division.

1. Medical review panels

If a worker or employer disagrees with a medical decision of an officer, the review board, or the Appeal Division, an appeal can be made to a medical review panel.

The worker's request for a review is termed a *grievance*. The most common issue considered by a medical review panel is whether the worker's condition is related to work. Back conditions are the most frequent injury assessed by the panels.

A certificate from a medical review panel is conclusive as to the medical issues stated in the certificate and cannot be reviewed or appealed.

The medical review panel consists of three physicians. A chairperson is appointed by the cabinet (Lieutenant Governor in Council) and two medical specialists are nominated by the worker and his or her employer. Each party receives a list of specialists from the board in the particular class of injury or disease for which the worker claims compensation. The panel must be appointed by the board within 18 days of the nominations and acceptance by the specialists.

To obtain a medical review panel, the employee, or his or her dependants, must send a grievance in writing, with particulars of the medical issue, to the board within 90 days of the medical decision, as well as a doctor's statement that there is a valid medical issue to be resolved.

An employer or former employer of a worker may make the same application if he or she disputes a medical decision of the board concerning the employee.

The purpose of the medical review panel is to conduct a physical examination of the worker, take the medical history, and review all board records. The panel then prepares a certificate and a narrative report that summarizes the medical file information and the findings of the panel in detail. The majority decision of the panel must be adopted by the board.

The certificate states:

(a) the medical condition of the worker,

(b) the existence or non-existence of the worker's disability,

(c) the nature and extent of any disability,

(d) the cause of the disability, and

(e) where the disability has more than one cause, how much of the disability is related to each cause.

2. The review board

The review board hears appeals from decisions made by a board officer. It consists of representatives of employers and workers, and chairpersons or vice chairpersons appointed by cabinet (the Lieutenant Governor in Council). Again, the goal is to have a balanced board which equally represents the interests of both parties.

A worker, or a deceased worker's surviving dependants, may appeal an officer's decision by filing a notice of appeal. The notice of appeal must be sent to the review board within 90 days of receipt of the letter from the Workers' Compensation Board that gives the officer's decision.

An employer may also appeal any decision of a claims officer.

The worker has a further six months to file particulars of the request for review. The particulars should state whether the worker wants an oral hearing or a review in which the board reads and reviews the officer's decision. The worker is present at the oral hearing. The worker is not present at the "read and review" but can submit written arguments.

The review board chooses which type of appeal is suitable. If the matter is not complex, the board can decide to make a decision based on a "read and review."

The claimant should state what remedy he or she wants from the review. Examples of possible remedies include the following:

(a) A request that wage loss benefits not be terminated

(b) A request to calculate average earnings on a different formula

(c) A request that the claim be accepted if the officer rejected the claim

(d) A request to increase the amount of the pension

The review board must give reasons in writing to the parties. Where the board allows a claim for compensation, payments must commence immediately.

A pamphlet that provides assistance on the format of the hearing, basic information, and a checklist on how to prepare an appeal is available from the board.

3. The appeal division

The appeal division is the next level of appeal. It hears appeals from the review board, as well as appeals by an employer against a penalty for violations of workplace health and safety standards or the amount of the assessment.

The appeal panels sit as one or three members. On a three-member panel, one member is an appeal commissioner, one represents workers, and one represents employers. Again, the appeal may be oral or written.

h. WORKERS' AND EMPLOYERS' ADVISERS

Workers often require assistance to file a claim for compensation or rehabilitation. Workers' advisers, paid by the government and operating independently of the Workers' Compensation Board, provide this assistance.

Advisers can give assistance to any worker or worker's dependant making a claim, unless they think the claim is without merit. An adviser can appear on behalf of the worker or his or her dependant before any board or tribunal.

Employers who disagree with an employee's claim can receive help from employers' advisers who perform the same duties.

Both advisers are entitled to access to the complete claims files of the board and any other material that relates to the worker's claim. This information must remain confidential.

i. EXCLUDED INDUSTRIES OR OCCUPATIONS

The purpose of the Workers' Compensation Act is to create a scheme of universal coverage, with exceptions only for exceptional industries or occupations whose circumstances do not fit the purpose and intent of the act.

Exemption orders will only be made for industrial or occupational groups, not to individual persons or businesses.

At the time of writing, the board has made exemption orders for only four types of workers:

(a) A person employed by the owner or occupier in or around a private residence, such as a domestic worker, who works for an average of less than:

    (i) eight hours per week, or

    (ii) 15 hours per week, where the person is employed caring for children in the period immediately preceding and following school

    (iii) a person employed to do a specific job or jobs involving a temporary period of less than 24 working hours

(b) Both spouses involved in unincorporated businesses where one or both own the business. ("Spouse" includes common-law and same-sex spouses. An exempt spouse can request voluntary coverage.)

(c) Non-resident employers and workers working temporarily in B.C. This applies only where an employer does not have a place of business in B.C. and is temporarily carrying on business in the province. The workers must not be resident in B.C.

(d) Professional sports competitors. This exemption does not include coaches, office, management or other support staff.

6
LABOUR CODE

Labour relations for most unionized workers and employers in B.C. are governed by the B.C. Labour Relations Code. Labour relations concerning federal employees and employers are governed by the Canada Labour Code.

The Labour Relations Code encourages peaceful and productive relationships between employers and unionized employees and protects the interests of the public by minimizing, where possible, the effects of any work stoppages. It tries to achieve a fair balance between the competing interests of union members and employers.

The objectives of the code are —

(a) to encourage the practice and procedure of collective bargaining between employers and trade unions as the freely chosen representatives of employees,

(b) to encourage co-operative participation between employers and trade unions in resolving workplace issues, adapting to changes in the economy, developing work force skills, and promoting workplace productivity,

(c) to minimize the effects of labour disputes on persons who are not involved in the disputes,

(d) to promote conditions favourable to the orderly, constructive, and expeditious settlement of disputes between employers and trade unions,

(e) to ensure that the public interest is protected during labour disputes, and

(f)   to encourage the use of mediation as a dispute resolution mechanism.

The act is administered by the Labour Relations Board, a
tribunal that consists of a chair, vice chairs, and other members. There are two divisions of the board: the mediation
division and the adjudication division. The purpose of the
mediation division is to work with the opposing parties in a
dispute to reach agreement. The purpose of the adjudication
division is to hear and determine disputes.

Matters are heard before a panel established by the chair.
Where members sit on the panel, there are equal member
representatives of employers and employees.

This chapter examines labour relations issues primarily from the perspective of the individual employee. It
describes the relationship between employees and both the
union and the employer, and the duties owed by a union
to an individual worker.

a.   EXCLUSIONS

Not every worker can choose to join a union. Federal employees, management employees, and independent contractors
are prohibited from membership in a B.C. union.

1.   Management employees

A management employee is a worker who is closely identified
with the owner of the workplace and has certain managerial
powers over other employees. For this group of employees,
membership in a union would create an unacceptable potential
conflict of interest. Collective bargaining between an employer
and a union must be conducted at arm's length. If an employee
has divided loyalties, or has information about the employer's
bargaining position, it would be unfair to permit that employee membership in a union.

The board has held that a particular employee may work
independently, but may still not be classified as a management

95

employee. The most important factors used by the board in determining that a person is a management employee are the authority to discipline or discharge employees, and labour relations input. Other factors considered include the following:

(a) The power to supervise the work of other employees

(b) The power to hire and to promote employees

(c) The power to authorize and to order overtime

(d) The power to evaluate employee performance

(e) The power to contribute to policy setting

2. Independent contractors

Traditional employees work regular hours for a single employer who determines their work conditions and requirements. Non-traditional workers contract their services to the employer. Contractors frequently work in the transportation and construction industries and are either independent or dependent. The distinction is important because independent contractors may not join unions, while dependent contractors have the right to join an existing union, or to form a separate unit of dependent contractors. These employees receive the same protections under the code as a traditionally employed worker.

The code defines a dependent contractor as someone who may or not be employed by a contract, and may furnish his or her own tools, etc., yet performs work or services for another person he or she is economically dependent on and under an obligation to perform duties for. The dependent contractor more closely resembles an employee than an independent contractor.

There are many applications to the board to determine whether workers are independent or dependent contractors. The test is whether the relationship between the employer and the contractor is one of economic dependency. A dependent contractor is in the labour market, not the product market. By contrast, an independent contractor offers both services and a product.

An example of an independent contractor is a plumber hired by an architect to install plumbing in a new home. The job is one of many for the plumber. There is no relationship of economic dependence between the plumber and the architect. An example of a dependent contractor is the owner and operator of a cement truck who delivers cement to various construction sites on the instructions of the manager of the cement plant. The truck driver owns his or her vehicle, but is economically dependent upon the work provided by the owner of the cement plant.

These factors may determine whether a worker is a dependent or independent contractor:

(a) Industry practice

(b) The nature of the work

(c) The employer's operation

(d) The type and extent of control exercised by the employer on issues such as hiring, firing, work assignment, and discipline

(e) The nature and manner of compensation

(f) The proportion of a contractor's income derived from a particular employer

(g) Whether the contractor advertises or solicits customers elsewhere

Example:

In 1994, the board considered whether certain taxi drivers were dependent contractors and eligible to join a union. Some drivers owned their vehicles, while others leased their vehicles. They worked for two closely associated companies at an airport.

The board held the drivers to be dependent contractors because the bulk of their income was derived from fares obtained from the airport taxi line, they did not hold taxi licences in their own right, they served the employer's customers, not their own customers, and the employer exercised significant control over them, including setting rules of operation and assignment of work on a daily basis.

3. Federal employees

Workers in federal undertakings are governed by the Canada Labour Code. Unionized workplaces are exempted from the Canada Labour Code's provisions concerning annual vacation, general holidays, bereavement leave, and minimum wages, where the collective agreement provides for better benefits.

b. HOW TO OBTAIN UNION REPRESENTATION

1. Certification

A group of non-unionized workers who wish to join a union should first talk with several unions to determine which one to join. Most industries and occupations have representation by a specific trade union. The best source of information about unions in B.C. is the B.C. Federation of Labour. A worker who wants to know how to form a union in his or her workplace can obtain all the necessary assistance from the federation.

Certification is the process by which a particular union is recognized by the board as the representative of a specific group of employees. Once a union is certified, it has the exclusive right to represent its members as a bargaining agent. A union remains the bargaining agent until it is decertified.

A union establishes sufficient support from workers in two ways. The union can sign up new members within 90 days prior to an application for certification as the union's bargaining agent. The union can also rely upon active union membership as demonstrated by payment of current union dues.

During a certification application, any employee who has sufficient continuing interest in the issue of union representation is eligible to vote. This can include short-term employees.

An organization drive initiates the certification process. Union members will meet with employees outside of working hours and attempt to persuade them to join their union.

2. Minimum number of union members

The union must prove that it has not less than 45% of the employees in a unit as members in good standing. The union can then apply to the board for certification for the unit.

Proof of membership is provided by a membership card which must be signed, dated at the time of the signature, and include the following statement:

> In applying for a membership I understand that the union intends to apply to be certified as my exclusive bargaining agent and to represent me in collective bargaining.

Where not less than 55% of the employees in the unit are members in good standing of the trade union, and the unit is appropriate for collective bargaining, the board shall certify the trade union as the employees' bargaining agent. No vote is required.

A representation vote will only be ordered by the board where not less than 45% and not more than 55% of the employees in a unit are members in good standing of a trade union. This vote is carried out under the supervision of the board, and all ballots are confidential.

3. Appropriate bargaining unit

Once a union has sufficient membership to apply for status as the bargaining agent for workers in a workplace, the next step is to establish the appropriateness of the proposed bargaining unit. The board favours a single bargaining unit for an employer if possible. The initial question upon certification is often whether the specific union that applies for certification on behalf of the employees is suitable both for those employees and for the employer.

For example, the employer may have several locations. The union will usually apply, if it has the necessary membership, to represent workers at all the locations in one single bargaining unit. Where a union applies for certification for a multiple location bargaining unit, it does not need to show 55% support at each location. The support must equal 55% in total.

To determine the appropriateness of a proposed bargaining unit, the board looks for a community of interest among the employees in question. The factors considered in determining this community of interest include the following:

(a) A similarity among employees of skills, interests, duties, and working conditions

(b) The physical and administrative structure of the employer

(c) Functional integration of work sites, if it is not a single site operation

(d) Geography

Where there is significant geographical separation among work sites, it may not be appropriate to certify one bargaining unit for all the work sites.

Sometimes a union applies to expand its existing bargaining unit by adding new employees. There must be majority support among the employees it proposes to add to the existing unit.

c. THE COLLECTIVE AGREEMENT

The collective agreement is a contract between the employer and the union representing the workers that defines the conditions of work, including wages, hours of work, overtime provisions, seniority provisions, and benefits.

The code provides that a trade union or employer shall not fail or refuse to bargain in good faith and to make every reasonable effort to conclude a collective agreement.

1. Requirements under the Employment Standards Act

The Employment Standards Act requires that the collective agreement contain provisions which meet its minimum standards to regulate the following:

(a) Hours of work and overtime

(b) Annual vacation and vacation pay

(c) Termination of employment or layoff

(d) Maternity and parental leave

However, the collective agreement may change these terms if it meets or exceeds the minimum requirements in one part of the act. For example, if the provisions for maternity and parental leave, considered together, meet or exceed the standards set out in the act, the parties may agree to provide greater parental leave in exchange for fewer days of maternity leave.

If a collective agreement contains any provision that does not satisfy the minimum requirements under the act, the Director of Employment Standards must be informed.

2. Requirements under the Labour Relations Code

The Labour Relations Code requires that the collective agreement contain these terms:

(a) A term of one year or more

(b) A provision governing the dismissal or discipline of employees covered by the agreement

(c) A term that an employer must have a just and reasonable cause for the dismissal or discipline of an employee covered by the agreement

(d) A provision for the final and conclusive settlement of disputes concerning the interpretation, application, operation, or alleged violation of the agreement, without work stoppage, by arbitration or another method

(e) A provision that requires either a consultation committee composed of the employer and the union representatives that consults regularly about issues relating to the workplace, or in the absence of such a provision, a meeting between these parties every two months to consult on workplace issues

(f) a provision that there will be no strikes or lockouts during the term of the agreement

These terms will be implied if they are not in the collective agreement.

3. Voluntary provisions

A collective agreement can include any other terms the employer and the trade union agree are appropriate, so long as the provisions of the Employment Standards Act are met.

One term often included is a requirement that all employees in a workplace that has a union certified as its bargaining agent be members of that union. This term can be a condition of employment. Another term the union may negotiate is a provision giving preference in employment to members of their union.

d. UNFAIR LABOUR PRACTICES BY EMPLOYERS

Every employee is guaranteed —

    (a) the freedom to belong to a trade union, and

    (b) the freedom to participate in lawful activities of the trade union.

The code recognizes that the time period when a union is organizing employees in a workplace is critical and that it is vital that the employer does not interfere during this time, which is called the certification drive.

Unfair labour practices include firing employees during this time period or providing special benefits to employees who do not join the union. During a certification drive, the employer cannot discharge, suspend, transfer, lay-off, or discipline any employee without proving just cause.

During collective bargaining, the terms and conditions of any expired collective agreement continue. The employer cannot alter any terms until a new collective agreement is signed or until the union loses its right to represent the employees.

An employer must always present any offers or bargaining positions to the union, not to individual employees.

A union can be automatically certified as the representative of the employees in a workplace as a result of unfair labour practices by the employer. Other remedies can be ordered when certification of the union is not appropriate. For example, an employer can be ordered to cease and desist from engaging in the unfair labour practice, to reimburse the union for any expenses in the organizational drive, or to reinstate a fired employee, or pay a former employee until he or she finds a suitable job.

Examples:

In a 1994 decision of the board, an employer was ordered to reinstate two former employees and pay union expenses for organizing the employees. The employer committed an unfair labour practice when it moved the unionized portion of its plant to Alberta shortly after the employer and the union signed the first collective agreement in B.C. The employer was found to be motivated in the decision to move the unionized portion of its plant to Alberta by anti-union sentiment.

The board ruled in another 1994 decision that an employer was clearly out of line when the employer conducted a vote among employees asking whether they supported a wage freeze. The employer also asked the employees if they would forego a wage increase provided for in the collective agreement. The employer had tried unsuccessfully to negotiate a wage freeze during the collective bargaining process.

Another example of an unfair labour practice by an employer occurred when, during a union's organizing drive, the employer posted a notice stating that promised wage increases would not be paid, due to the presence of the union in the workplace. The remedy ordered was that the union be certified to represent the employees.

Another example of an unfair labour practice occurred during an organizational campaign by a union to receive status as a bargaining agent for a group of employees. During an employee meeting of some workers who did not wish to join the union, a mill superintendent promised a wage increase. The board held that the mill superintendent was clearly a representative of the employer and found employer interference with the union's right to organize.

e. MEDIATION

Mediation is the process by which the employer and a union use a mediation officer to help them reach a first collective agreement or renew the current collective agreement.

The purpose of mediation is to arrive at mutual agreement between the parties concerning any issues in conflict. Either the employer or the union can request the appointment of a mediation officer by making the request in writing to the associate chair of the mediation division of the Labour Relations Board.

The Minister of Labour can appoint a mediation officer at any time during the course of collective bargaining. A fact finder can also be appointed during a collective bargaining dispute to meet with the employer and the union representatives to define those matters that are in dispute and those on which the parties agree.

f. ARBITRATION

Arbitration is when a labour dispute arising under a collective agreement can be settled by order of the arbitration board. The difference between mediation and arbitration is that mediation is voluntary. The parties may disagree with the conclusions of the mediator. By contrast, the decision of the arbitration board is binding on the employer and the union.

The purpose of arbitration is to resolve grievances and disputes without work stoppages that effect both the parties and the public. The Collective Agreement Arbitration Bureau of the board, which consists of a director and settlement officers, administers the arbitration process.

1. Arbitration provisions in collective agreements

All collective agreements must contain two important provisions:

(a) a provision requiring the employer to have a just and reasonable cause for the dismissal or discipline of an employee, and

(b) a provision for the settlement of disputes concerning the interpretation application or alleged violation of the collective agreement by arbitration or another method which is final and conclusive without work stoppage.

These provisions are deemed to be in any collective agreement that does not expressly contain them.

2. Request for arbitration

A dispute begins with a grievance. For example, a worker is disciplined by an employer for failing to work a weekend shift. The union files a grievance about the disciplinary action. After the grievance procedure is complete, according to the terms of the collective agreement, if the union is not satisfied with the employer's action, it can request that the director of the arbitration board appoint a settlement officer. The employer can also request the appointment of a settlement officer.

The request should be in writing and state the issue to be determined. If the director appoints a settlement officer, he or she must —

(a) inquire into the difference between the parties,

(b) try to assist them in settling the difference, and

(c) report to the director the results of his or her efforts.

The board may also order arbitration where there has been a delay in settling a difference, or it is a source of industrial unrest.

3. Powers of the arbitration board

The arbitration board can make the following decisions concerning a dispute that arises under a collective agreement:

(a) Order that one person pay another person damages for the injury or loss suffered

(b) Order that an employer reinstate an employee dismissed in contravention of the collective agreement (Usually, this means an employee dismissed without just cause.)

(c) Order that the employer or trade union rescind and correct any disciplinary action taken that violates the collective agreement

The board has other powers to assist the parties in reaching a settlement, but these three orders are the most frequent results of arbitration.

4. Expedited arbitration

The employer or the union can refer an unresolved issue to the director for expedited arbitration. This means that a hearing must be held within 28 days, and a decision given within 21 days of the hearing.

Expedited arbitration takes place only after any grievance procedure has been exhausted and must be requested within 45 days of the completion of the grievance procedure.

g. DISPUTES

Mediation and arbitration are not always successful. Work stoppages may occur when no consensus can be reached between the employer and the union about the terms of the collective agreement. The union may choose to cease work and strike; the employer may choose to lock out the employees from the work site.

1. A strike

A strike normally consists of cessation of all work by union employees. It can also include a concerted refusal by all employees to work overtime in an attempt to limit production. The purpose of a strike is to exert economic pressure on the employer by withdrawing worker services to compel the employer to agree to terms in a proposed collective agreement.

Strikes are prohibited during the term of the collective agreement. A lawful strike can only take place once the agreement's term expires.

(a) The strike vote

A strike vote must be held prior to any strike. The employees in the unit affected will vote according to terms of the code's regulations. For the vote to pass, a majority of the employees voting must vote in favour of a strike.

The voting procedure requires a secret ballot and the vote will be supervised by a returning officer appointed by the union. The results, called the poll return, must be sent promptly to the associate chair of the Mediation Division of the board.

If that vote is in favour of a strike, any strike must occur within three months of that vote.

(b) Strike requirements

After the majority of employees vote in favour of a strike, there cannot be a lawful strike until —

(a) the trade union serves written notice to the employer that the employees are going on strike,

(b) the trade union files written notice to the board of the intended strike, and

(c) 72 hours or more have passed since notice is given.

(c) Appointment of a mediation officer

The associate chair of the mediation division can appoint a mediation officer once notice of the intended strike is given to the board. The mediation officer meets with the employer and the trade union and attempts to resolve the bargaining dispute.

The officer reports back to the associate chair no later than ten days after meeting with the parties, or 20 days after their appointment.

(d) Perishable property

The board can require the union to give more than 72 hours' notice if perishable property, or other property or persons affected by perishable property, will need protection. This extended notice period allows the employer time to make arrangements to move or otherwise deal with the perishable property prior to the strike.

Perishable property includes property such as food that can spoil quickly or become dangerous to life, health, or other property.

2. Lockout

A lockout is defined as closing a place of employment, a suspension of work, or a refusal by an employer to continue to employ of number of his or her employees. Its purpose is to compel the employees to agree to conditions of employment.

The pre-lockout requirements are the same as for a strike. The employer must —

(a) serve written notice on the trade union of the intended lockout,

(b) file written notice of the intended lockout with the board, and

(c) wait 72 hours before the lockout commences.

The rules concerning the appointment of a mediation officer are discussed under the strike provisions (see **g. 1.** above).

The employer cannot use replacement workers after locking out the union employees.

3. Essential services

Certain services necessary to the health, safety, or welfare of the residents of B.C. cannot be withdrawn in a strike. These are termed "essential services."

Before or during a work stoppage, the Minister of Labour can direct the board to designate certain services as essential. Once a service is designated essential, such as emergency hospital care, the unionized employees must continue to work even if their bargaining unit is on strike.

Once the board orders that certain services are essential, the union, not the employer, has the responsibility of scheduling members to work in an essential service area.

4. Picketing

Picketing is defined as attending at or near a person's place of business, operations, or employment to persuade or attempt to persuade anyone not to —

    (a) enter that place of business, operations, or employment,

    (b) deal in or handle that person's products, or

    (c) do business with that person.

A union during a lawful strike or lockout pickets the workplace in order to exert economic pressure on the employer. Where the union wishes to picket a site shared with other employers, and innocent third parties will be affected, the board can regulate the terms and place of picketing.

5. Replacement workers

The purpose of a lawful strike or lockout is to exert economic pressure against the other party. The use of replacement workers during a labour dispute is prohibited. This is a new and important protection for trade unions.

A replacement worker is anyone who provides services which were performed by the unionized workers who have withdrawn their services, or were locked out by the employer.

The code states that during an authorized lockout or strike, an employer shall not use the services of a person, whether paid or not —

    (a) who is hired or engaged after the date the notice to commence collective bargaining is given or the date on which bargaining begins,

    (b) who ordinarily works at another of the employer's places of operations,

    (c) who is transferred to a place of operations where the strike or lockout is taking place, if he or she was transferred after the date the notice to commence

110

bargaining is given or the date on which bargaining begins, or

(d) who is employed, engaged, or supplied to the employer by another person.

An employer can't take any job action against an employee not on strike who refuses to replace a striking worker. For example, management workers are not union members, but have the right to refuse any request by their employer to take over duties performed by a union member. This includes intimidation in any form including threatening dismissal or terminating the employee.

h. JOINT CONSULTATION COMMITTEE

Each collective agreement must provide for a consultation committee at the request of either the employer or trade union after notice to commence collective bargaining is given. A collective agreement that does not contain such a provision is deemed to contain this provision:

> On the request of either party, the parties shall meet at least once every two months until this agreement is terminated for the purpose of discussing issues relating to the workplace that affect the parties or any employee bound by this agreement.

The purpose of a consultation committee is to encourage a more co-operative relationship between management and the trade union and to provide for mid-contract consultation about workplace issues and changes in the economy.

i. ADJUSTMENT PLAN

Another labour code requirement that encourages co-operation between the employer and the trade union is the development of an adjustment plan. When an employer makes substantial changes to policy or practice that affect a significant number of members of a bargaining unit, an adjustment plan must be developed by the union and the employer.

The purpose of an adjustment plan is to develop a plan for instituting these changes in the workplace. For example, the employer may wish to implement technological changes that will result in a need for fewer employees. An adjustment plan will try to minimize the potential impact of these changes on job security.

The employer must notify the union 60 days or more prior to making any substantial changes to the terms, conditions, or security of employment.

An adjustment plan developed by the employer and the trade union can include provisions respecting any of the following:

(a) Consideration of alternatives to the proposed measure, policy, practice, or change, including amendment of provisions in the collective agreement

(b) Human resources planning and employee counselling and retraining

(c) Notice of termination

(d) Severance pay

(e) Entitlement to pension and other benefits

(f) A process to oversee the implementation of the adjustment plan

j. THE UNION'S DUTIES TO THE EMPLOYEE

An employee in a trade union gives up any right to bargain directly with the employer about work conditions in return for the protections offered by the union.

However, a union represents the individual as well as the group. It owes several fundamental duties to any person or to any employee in the bargaining unit the union represents. It must satisfy the principles of natural justice in all internal union affairs, and it must not act in a manner that is arbitrary, discriminatory, or in bad faith.

1. The duty of fair representation

A union that is certified to represent workers in an appropriate bargaining unit acts on behalf of the interests of the workers as a whole. However, it also owes a duty of fair representation to individual employees. Sometimes, these two duties conflict.

For example, a union may advance the interests of more senior employees over less senior employees as part of its mandate to protect job security through seniority rights. This may be appropriate, but the union must always represent the individual employee fairly as well. Each employee has given up any right to bargain directly with the employer about working conditions in return for union representation. In return, the union must fairly represent each employee in the bargaining unit.

However, certain preferences of one employee over another are permitted under the code. For example, it is not a violation for a trade union to enter into an agreement under which an employer is permitted to hire by name certain trade union members. Nor is it a violation to provide preferential hiring to trade union members resident in a particular geographic area.

(a) How to complain

An employee who thinks the union violated this duty of fair representation should file a written complaint with the board. The board then determines whether or not the complaint discloses a sufficient case to require an answer. If so, an inquiry will begin.

Notice of the complaint is served on the union. An officer may be appointed to inquire into the details of the complaint and to try to settle the matter. He or she reports the results of the inquiry to the board. If a settlement is not possible, the board may inquire into the complaint.

The board, when examining whether the union violated its duty of fair representation to the employee who filed the complaint, reviews the union's conduct during the entire grievance and arbitration process. The issue is whether the union made a thoughtful and reasoned judgment about the employee's grievance.

For example, a union may agree with an employer that the termination of a specific employee is justified. The union then chooses not to arbitrate the dismissal. If the board determines that the union did not demonstrate bad faith or discrimination and did not act arbitrarily, its decision will be upheld.

(b) Remedies

If, after an inquiry, the board is satisfied that the union violated its duty of fair representation, it can direct the union to cease doing any prohibited act or to correct any act.

2. The duty of fairness

The union must act fairly in matters concerning disputes about the constitution of the union or union membership. The code states that every person has a right to the application of the principles of natural justice in all disputes relating to various aspects of the trade union.

Natural justice is the duty to act fairly when reaching an administrative decision. The principles of natural justice can include many procedural protections, such as the right to be given notice and the opportunity to be heard when a decision will be made which can affect a person.

For example, a union has powers, in its internal constitution, to discipline union members. The principles of natural justice require that when a union disciplines a member, that member must be informed of the issue and given an opportunity to respond.

Suspension or expulsion from a trade union for an alleged breach of its internal rules has important consequences for an employee. If the union has an agreement with the employer that union membership is a requirement of employment, the person not only loses union membership, he or she also loses employment.

3. How to complain

The procedure to complain of a union's breach of the principles of natural justice is the same procedure used for complaints that a union breached its duty of fair representation. The worker files a written complaint with the board.

Notice of the complaint is served on the union. An officer may be appointed to inquire into the details of the complaint, and to try to settle the matter. The officer then reports the results of any inquiry to the board.

If settlement is not possible, the board can examine the complaint, and if it is valid, order a remedy.

4. Remedies

The board, if satisfied that the union has unfairly expelled, suspended, or imposed a penalty on a person, can order the union to reinstate that person to union membership and to pay them:

(a) a sum equal to any wages lost due to the wrongful suspension or expulsion, and

(b) the amount of any wrongful penalty or fee assessment.

The board can also order the union to cease any prohibited act of unfairness against a person and to rectify the consequences of such an act.

k. RELIGIOUS EXEMPTION

Union membership is usually compulsory once a trade union is certified as the bargaining agent for a unit of employees.

The collective agreement often requires all employees to be members of the union and/or pay union dues.

However, the code recognizes that an individual's personal religious beliefs may prohibit union membership or prohibit the paying of dues or assessments to trade unions generally. (Political or social beliefs which are anti-union do not constitute grounds for exemption from union membership.)

The employee must satisfy the board that religious beliefs prohibit membership in or the payment of dues in any union, not simply the particular union in the employee's workplace.

1. Application for exemption from union membership

The employee should apply in writing to the board for exemption from union membership, under section 17 of the code.

The application should include —

(a) the religious group to which the applicant belongs,

(b) the reason for the request on religious grounds, and

(c) a supporting letter from another member of the religious group that states the group's beliefs, and the writer's understanding of the applicant's beliefs.

An officer of the board will interview the applicant, the employer, and other parties such as union officials. Any interested party, including the union, can oppose the application for membership exemption.

2. Terms of an order for exemption

Once the board receives and considers the application, if it is satisfied about the validity of the applicant's religious beliefs, it can order one of the following:

(a) That the employee is not required to join a trade union

(b) That the employee is not required to continue to be a member of a trade union

(c) That the employee is not liable to pay any dues, fees, or assessments to the trade union

(d) That amounts equal to these fees be paid by the employee, or the employer on their behalf, to a charitable organization registered under Part I of the Income Tax Act

A person exempted from union membership due to religious beliefs may not vote in any vote conducted by a trade union such as a strike vote, or in a vote held for the purposes of the code.

1. THE DUTY TO ACCOMMODATE

The employer and the trade union must accommodate an employee's religious or other beliefs protected under human rights legislation.

Discrimination on the part of a trade union includes both the inclusion of a term in a collective agreement that directly discriminates against an employee or impedes the reasonable efforts of an employer to accommodate religious beliefs.

Example:

The Supreme Court of Canada considered the duty to accommodate in 1993. A school board custodian who belonged to the union could not work from sundown Friday until sundown Sunday according to his religious beliefs. The school board created a special shift for the employee to permit his religious observance.

The union threatened to file a grievance because the special shift violated the terms of the collective agreement and the employee was fired. The court decided that any collective agreement must be subject to the Human Rights Code. The test to be applied in terms of the union's duty to accommodate a member's religious beliefs is one of reasonableness. Here, the union breached its duty to accommodate a member's protected religious beliefs.

APPENDIX
ADDRESSES AND TELEPHONE NUMBERS

a. EMPLOYMENT STANDARDS BRANCH OFFICES

These offices give assistance to non-unionized workers and unionized workers. They answer inquiries about the Employment Standards Act and the Labour Relations Act.

The information publication, *Employment Standards Information Bulletin,* can be obtained from these offices.

Abbotsford
306 - 32555 Simon Avenue
V2T 4Y7
853-5378

Burnaby
Deer Lake Centre
Suite 210, 4946 Canada Way
V5G 4J6
660-4000

Courtenay
2500 Cliffe Avenue
V9N 3P9
426-1291

Dawson Creek
1201 - 103rd Avenue
V1G 4J2
784-2390

Kamloops
220 - 546 St. Paul Street
V2C 5T1
828-4516

Kelowna
107 - 1664 Richter Street
V1Y 8N3
861-7404

Nanaimo
155 Skinner Street
V9R 5E8
755-2342

Nelson
310 Ward Street
V1L 5S4
354-6550

Penticton
103 - 3547 Skaha Lake Road
V2A 7K2
492-1333

Port Coquitlam
510 - 2755 Lougheed Highway
V3B 5Y9
565-6120

Prince George
1044 - 5th Avenue
V2L 5G4
565-6120

Surrey
210 - 5569 176th Street
V3S 4C2
576-1323

Terrace
108 - 3220 Eby Street
V8G 5K8
638-3272

Vernon
3201 - 30th Street
V1T 9G3
549-5664

Victoria
3rd Floor 1019 Wharf Street
V8V 1X4
387-1220

Williams Lake
540 Borland Street
V2G 1R8
398-4478

b. HUMAN RIGHTS OFFICES

Complaints and information concerning human rights issues can be obtained from the Employment Standards Branch offices listed above. The toll-free number is: 1-800-663-0876

c. WORKERS' COMPENSATION OFFICES

1. Workers' Adviser

The Workers' Adviser assists workers or their dependants on all Workers' Compensation claims.

Richmond
3000 - 8171 Ackroyd Road
V6X 3K1
660-7888
1-800-663-4261 (toll free)

Prince George
510 - 550 Victoria Street
V2L 2K1
565-4280
1-800-263-6066 (toll free)

Victoria
314 - 3995 Quadra Street
V8X 1J8
953-4608
1-800-661-4066 (toll free)

2. Employers' Adviser

The Employers' Adviser assists employers and potential employers with claims under the Workers' Compensation Act and occupational health or safety issues.

Richmond
4003 - 8171 Ackroyd Road
V6X 3K1
660-7253

Prince George
512 - 550 Victoria Street
V2L 2K1
525-4285

3. Workers' Compensation Review Board

200 - 1700 West 75th Avenue
Vancouver, B.C.
V6P 6G2
1-800-663-2782 (toll free)

d. LABOUR RELATIONS BOARD

The board mediates and resolves labour disputes under the Labour Relations Code.

> 1125 Howe Street
> Vancouver
> V6Z 2K8
> 660-1300

e. APPRENTICESHIP PROGRAMS

The Apprenticeship Board oversees the standards for apprenticeship training in B.C.

> 244 - 4299 Canada Way
> Burnaby
> V5G 1H3
> 436-0317

The Skills Development Centres set standards and provide certification for apprenticeship training.

> **Abbotsford**
> 105 - 2975 Gladwin Road
> V2S 6W8
> 825-5922

> **Burnaby**
> 200 - 4946 Canada Way
> V5G 4J6
> 660-7100

> **Coquitlam**
> 3039 Anson Avenue
> V3B 2H6
> 775-0778

> **Cranbrook**
> 201 - 117 10th Avenue South
> V1C 2N1
> 426-1281

Dawson Creek
104 - 1508 102nd Avenue
V1G 2E2
784-2388

Kamloops
236 St. Paul Street
V2C 6G4
828-4522

Kelowna
200 - 1626 Richter Street
V1Y 2M3
861-7407

Prince George
211 - 1577 Seventh Avenue
V2L 3P5
565-6020

Surrey
102 - 9030 King George VI Highway
V3V 7Y3
660-8944

Terrace
3250 Eby Street
V8G 5H4
638-3211

Vancouver
133 East Eighth Avenue
V5T 1R8
660-6272

Victoria
First Floor, 838 Fort Street
V8V 1X4
387-3698

f. CANADA LABOUR RELATIONS BOARD

800 Burrard Street
Suite 1660
Vancouver, B.C.
V6Z 2G7
666-6001

If you have enjoyed this book and would like to receive a free catalogue of all Self-Counsel titles, please write to:

Self-Counsel Press
1481 Charlotte Road
North Vancouver, B.C.
V7J 1H1